Your Baby's First 30 Months

Lucie W. Barber, Ed.D.,
Director of Applied Research,
Union College Character Research Project

Herman Williams, M.Th.,
Director,
Union College Character Research Project

Your Baby's First 30 Months is based on research undertaken during the past 30 years at the Union College Character Research Project in Schenectady, New York. UCCRP has pioneered research in positive mental health. It has developed educational methods for parents, especially those who are the main educators of their child. The goal of the program is to promote healthy attitudes and values in the family.

Publishers: Bill and Helen Fisher
Executive Editor: Carl Shipman
Editorial Director: Jonathan Latimer
Editor: Randy Summerlin
Art Director: Don Burton
Book Design & Assembly: Tom Jakeway
Typography: Cindy Coatsworth, Joanne Nociti and Michelle Claridge
Major Photography: Diane Ensign-Caughey and Don Gennett
Additional Photography: Scott Millard, Neal Wilson and parents of children in Character Research Project.
Cover Photograph: Robin Forbes

H.P. Books, P.O. Box 5367, Tucson, AZ 85703   (602) 888-2150
ISBN: 0-89586-062-7
Library of Congress Catalog Card Number: 81-80307
©1981 Fisher Publishing, Inc. Printed in U.S.A.

My name is _____

(Place your baby's photograph here)

This picture of me was taken _____
(date)

I was born _____
(year, month, day, hour and minute)

at _____
(place of birth and address)

I live at _____
(home address)
_____

My parents are: **Father:** _____

     Mother: _____

The other members of my family (brothers, sisters and others living in the same house) are:

Name	Birth date	Relationship
_____	_____	_____
_____	_____	_____
_____	_____	_____
_____	_____	_____

Contents

About This Book **5**

Months 1 & 2 .... **7**
How to establish a lasting bond with your child. Understand your baby's fascination with faces, grasp reflex and emotional reflexes. Learn to interpret communicative cries.
Father's Role **14**
Chart Your Child's Progress **16**

Months 3 & 4 .... **25**
Enjoy your child's social smile and growing curiosity. Vision, eye-hand coordination and social skills improve. Delight in your child's babbling and cooing.
The Working Mother **33**
Chart Your Child's Progress **34**

Months 5—7 .... **43**
Your child develops a memory and eats more solid food. Babyproof the house for safety. Baby learns to drop and throw. First teeth appear.
Right and Wrong **53**
Chart Your Child's Progress **54**

Months 8—12 .... **63**
Your child is more active. Take a break and hire a baby sitter. Teach your child what "no" means. Possible first words and steps.
Discovering Sexuality **76**
Selecting Toys **78**
Chart Your Child's Progress **80**

Months 13—16 .... **89**
Play "see and learn" games. Help your toddler with hand development and social skills. Watch for nonverbal communication. Comfort child when fearful and frustrated.
Discipline **102**
Chart Your Child's Progress **104**

Months 17—24 .... **113**
Improved small muscles make dressing and undressing easier. Prepositions, pronouns and use of names appear in your child's language. Running and jumping improve. Time to see dentist.
Toilet Training **126**
Chart Your Child's Progress **128**

Months 25—30 .... **137**
Self-confident child develops a greater imagination. Learns by looking and fitting things together. Your child may be affectionate, but inconsistent.
Your Child's Positive Self-Image **147**
Chart Your Child's Progress **148**
The Future **156**

Sources of Information, Index **158, 159**

Learning to smile is an early part of social training.

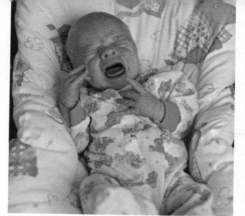

Crying is your baby's way of telling you he needs something.

Birthday party: A symbol of growth and accomplishment.

About this Book

What you accomplish in the first 30 months as a parent will serve as a guide for the rest of your child's life. To be successful, *you must get to know your child well.* That's what this book is all about.

Thirty months sounds like a long time, but it's short compared to a life expectancy of 70 years. Treasure these precious months when your son or daughter is a baby and a toddler. *Get to know this unique person who is your own dear child.*

We have chosen to write about your child's first 30 months because that covers *infancy.* Behavior and development is more *predictable* in these months. By the end of 30 months we have gone beyond infancy to the *early childhood* stage. Development is much more *variable* after the first 30 months.

WATCH YOUR CHILD AND LEARN

This book is about your child's growth and development, and about the art of parenting. It will challenge you to become an *active learner.* This process involves more than mere reading. It

Your baby may be vocal and outgoing at first, then become quiet and pensive, like the toddler at left. Get to know your child well in the first 30 months. This will increase the joys and ease the tasks of parenthood.

calls for careful observation and attention to your child. You are urged to fill in the learning and observation charts at the end of each chapter.

You can keep records in the spaces provided. By doing so, you will become more intimately aware of your child's growth. Get involved in recording your baby's skills and behavior. Evaluate what you observe. Then you'll know much more about your child.

KEEP CHARTS

Charts in this book vary. Some call for keeping daily or weekly records; others are monthly. They will be most effective if you attend to them regularly.

Methodical recordkeeping will help you learn about your baby and deepen your relationship. It will also serve as a valuable, permanent source of background information about your child. At the end of 30 months of careful recordkeeping, you'll have a book full of laughs, warm memories and probably a few tears!

30 YEARS OF RESEARCH

We have avoided technical, academic language. Our book is based on more than 30 years of careful, formal research about parents and children. This material was gathered by the Union College Character Research Project in Schenectady, N.Y.

YOUR CHILD IS AN INDIVIDUAL

Chapters treat each age range with a regular sequence of growth and development subsections. This gives you a step-by-step look at how an *average* child *might* develop from birth through 30 months.

One word of advice about studying average statistics: *Neither your child, nor your neighbor's, nor any other child will develop at exactly the same rate.* The so-called average child is a myth. Bear in mind as you read this book and grow with your child that his personality is *unique.* Pay attention to *his* development. Don't be tempted to compare him with another child's progress in walking or talking.

HE AND SHE

We have attempted to personalize this book for you and your child. This has presented the problem of calling children "he" or "she" and "him" or "her." We refuse to call a child "it." Our solution has been to use male or female pronouns in alternating chapters. However, when we use "he" we mean either a boy or a girl. Same applies when we use "she."

We begin each chapter with a Baby Talk section to help you understand your child's point of view about life. If your baby could speak, this is what he might say about his needs in coming months.

Baby Talk

So this is the real world. I can see that life is going to be fun!

I admit, I've had it pretty easy up to now. I guess I owe you an apology for these first few weeks. All I really want to do is eat and sleep.

Before I was born it was nice having a Mother to give me everything I needed. But now I have to learn to tell you what I want. I can't do a thing for myself.

I'm happy that you're here to keep me comfortable and help me adjust to my new surroundings. I love it when you hold me, touch me, cuddle me and talk to me!

That's the best way I know to feel close to you.

The comfort of being in your arms and looking into your eyes makes me feel good. In a few weeks I'll be smiling!

I cry a lot these days. That's just my way of talking to you. If I sometimes come on a little strong and seem upset, don't worry. I'm probably just hungry, or maybe I need a diaper change.

I'm just thankful I have you here when I need you. I'm especially glad you're listening to me as I learn to communicate my needs.

You know, I'm starting to like this. I'm delighted that we're partners. Thanks!

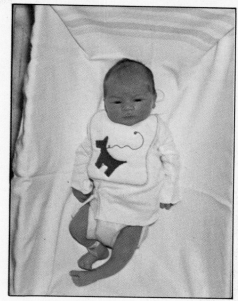

Your newborn depends on you for survival.

Looking Ahead

Your baby is virtually helpless and almost totally dependent on you. He may seem small and fragile, but he's tougher than you think.

Babies need adequate physical care: warmth, cleanliness, food and rest. For the first few months, give your baby these essentials. He'll develop naturally and normally. Don't be afraid that you'll do something wrong or that your lack of experience as a parent will harm your child. Your influence on the baby is important. While he's developing his basic abilities, don't be concerned about making mistakes.

You face a busy challenge that may seem hectic in the coming months. Getting to know your new baby will be easier and more

---

Your first priority: Establish a bond, or emotional attachment, between you, your baby and the family.

---

joyful if you relax as you progress through parenthood.

As you read through this book, remember that when we say "he" or "she" we mean any child regardless of sex.

BONDING

Your first task in learning how to be a parent is already at hand. A close personal bond should be established between you, your child and others in the family. *Bonding, or emotional attachment, develops by close contact: holding and cuddling, gazing deeply into baby's eyes, skin-to-skin contact and plenty of talking.* If the whole family has close physical contact with your new child, bonding will occur naturally.

DEVELOPING TRUST

Your second major concern during the first two months is helping your baby learn to trust you. He arrived from the safe, relative quiet of Mother's body into a strange, loud and frightening new world. *He must discover that his world is not so terrifying after all.*

He must learn that you will meet his needs for food and attention. His level of trust will increase as you show him you care.

Parents often ask, "Can I spoil my baby if I jump at his every demand?" Don't worry about spoiling your child during the first two months of his life. He *must* have certain requirements met. You won't teach him to be demanding or spoil him when you anticipate and meet his genuine needs.

Meeting your baby's *genuine* needs is the tricky part. You will not succeed unless you pay close attention to what your baby is trying to tell you. You must consider the common causes of crying: Does he want to be fed? Does he need to be changed out of wet or dirty clothes? Does he need to be moved to a new position?

When your baby cries, check out all the needs you can think of: hunger, discomfort with diapers, clothes or position. Check discomfort with temperature, fright from sudden noises or bright lights or the need for sleep. You will not spoil your baby. By paying attention you'll soon learn to distinguish cries that signify different problems.

One need of newborn babies may not be readily apparent: *Some babies genuinely must have a good cry.* If you have checked the usual problems and your baby still cries, consider that he may need to exercise his respiratory muscles.

Some babies are born with underdeveloped muscles that control breathing. They need to cry to develop these muscles. If they do not cry they may have trouble breathing. So check all ordinary needs and if nothing works, don't feel guilty about letting your baby cry for 10 or 15 minutes. If he cries longer, check him again.

SPECIAL NEEDS

During the first two months, your baby has some important requirements that are simple to fulfill:

Comfort—Warmth and security of the womb have come and gone for your baby. In his harsh new world, he has a strong *urge for peace.* This can be supplied by your own calm and cheer. You must learn from your child what kind of clothing he finds comfortable. Some children like snug diapers, clothing and bed linens. Others resist tight clothing and prefer to have their hands free and blankets loose.

Schedule—Much has been said about schedules for babies. In the 1940s parents were urged to adhere to a four-hour feeding schedule. Then came a swing to total permissiveness: Feed the baby whenever the baby cries. This didn't work very well because not all cries mean hunger.

Now researchers have found that 40 percent of babies adjust to a regular schedule easily and quickly. Ten percent have irregular sleep and eating schedules. Another 15 percent simply take longer to settle into a schedule than the first

Your baby's ability to suck is a natural reflex. He'll suck enthusiastically when he's hungry and stop when he's full or when he falls asleep. Feeding time is an important occasion to develop the close bond between mother and baby. Breast-feeding babies get an extra bonus: They feel the warmth and closeness of mother's body.

group. The remaining 35 percent of babies could not be classified according to schedule.

This leads to a good lesson: *Don't try to classify your baby.* Your child is one-of-a-kind. Your challenge is to find the best schedule for your baby by paying attention to what he's trying to say.

It may help you to keep records of sleeping times and waking times on page 18. You may discover patterns emerging. Records can help you adapt to changes in your baby's schedule as he grows older.

Communication—Your new baby is only vaguely aware of your existence. His attempt to communicate begins almost immediately. The language of infancy is what we call *crying.* The physical activity of a baby can tell you about his needs and feelings. His cry has different sounds and rhythms, meaning different things at different times. Parents who pay close attention to their child's behavior and crying can begin to interpret his primitive infant language. Keep a written record of your baby's cries on page 21 to help you understand his language.

About Your Child

Every baby has a unique personality. Your baby is different from every other. He's an original!

Along with his genetic inheritance, your child's experiences before and during birth have combined to make him like no other. At birth he begins to express his uniqueness.

Some children are born into the world "kicking and screaming." They are often irritable and easily disturbed. They may not sleep well and cry a lot. This fretful behavior may have no apparent cause. Parents whose children behave this way often feel guilty about their lack of parenting skills. They feel that if they were *competent,* their child would not be so miserable.

Other babies are easily startled or frightened by loud noises or sudden bright lights. Some infants are easily awakened.

Sleepy babies seem to have an almost unlimited capacity for sleep. They sometimes have to be awakened for feeding and immediately go back to sleep. Parents of these babies often brag that their child already sleeps through the night.

Some infants are extremely wakeful. They seem to be alert and ready to participate in everything. They may demand more attention than others.

Infants differ widely, just as adults do. You must recognize your child's own personality. There is no typical behavior that describes a child during the first two months. *You must observe your baby.* He's telling you a lot about himself.

He's saying, "Pay attention to me!" It may be one of the most important messages you and your child will ever exchange.

Mouth and Eyes

Your baby spends a lot of time eating. The function of his mouth at mealtime is important. Meals are highlights of his day.

SUCKING REFLEX

When your baby takes food from a breast or bottle, sucking is an automatic reflex. No conscious decision is necessary. If you touch your child's cheek, his mouth will open and his head will turn in an attempt to suck your finger.

This built-in sucking reflex becomes a learning exercise for your baby. He'll suck vigorously when hungry, usually slowing down as his hunger subsides. Sucking will become infrequent and sporadic as he completes feeding and gets sleepy.

Your child may pause during sucking when he is several weeks old. Pauses become intentional as his attention is captured by bright colors or by your face. This staring at interesting objects represents one of his first conscious acts. Up to now, everything done by your

baby was a reflex. Now he's beginning to choose whether to suck or to look!

NEARSIGHTED VISION

At this age your baby is extremely nearsighted. Objects 8 to 10 inches from his eyes are in clear focus. Everything at a greater distance is blurred or hazy. Blank stares indicate that distant objects are out of focus. Place colorful objects such as sheets, blankets, towels or clothing close to your baby's eyes and he'll perk up. *A mobile hung on the crib or wall will not interest a young infant. It is too far away to be seen clearly.*

When objects are 8 to 10 inches from your baby's face, he'll distinguish those that interest him. Some babies prefer certain colors and shapes. *You can learn much about your child's preferences by showing him different shapes and colors.* Then record which he prefers.

A young baby has amazingly good vision, but he can't see far yet. Distant objects are blurred for the first few weeks. By 2 months

of age, his nearsightedness will subside. He can then see as far as the door. He'll look toward the door when he hears someone approaching.

There may be a reason for his initial nearsightedness. Eight to ten inches corresponds to the distance between your eyes and the baby's eyes when he is nursing or taking a bottle. Eye-to-eye contact is important as your baby forms a bond with you and other members of the family.

FASCINATION WITH FACES

Infants appear to be fascinated by the human face. Your baby will scan any object resembling a face that comes within his view. Usually he'll begin at the hairline, moving down to the chin. Then he'll focus on the eyes.

Fascination with the form of the face is more than idle activity. Babies will often stare intensely into the eyes of another person for long periods. Staring is one means of establishing the personal bond between parent and child that we mentioned earlier. When your

A young baby's vision is limited during the first few weeks. He can focus on objects 8 to 10 inches away. Anything farther will be blurred. If you hang mobiles in the crib to interest your child, be sure they are within his range of vision.

Human faces, or even rough drawings like that above, will capture a young baby's attention. Show your baby this one, or create a larger version. Then watch his reaction!

baby is feeding, the connection between hunger satisfaction and the pleasure of looking into your eyes strengthens this bond.

Manipulation

During the first two months, arm and hand actions are almost totally controlled by reflexes. He will not discover his hands for several more weeks.

GRASP REFLEX

Hand and foot reflexes will disappear as your baby learns to use these parts of his body. The *grasp reflex* can be seen easily in young infants. Touch baby's palm with your finger and his fingers will tightly grasp yours. This grip is so strong that premature and newborn infants can be lifted by the strength of their own grip. *But don't lift your baby in this manner.* The reflex will disappear during the first few months and an unexpected fall could occur.

The same reflex can be seen with your baby's toes. Stroke the sole of his foot with your finger. He'll flex his toes around your finger. Like the hand reflex, the toe grip suddenly disappears during the first few months.

The grasp reflex can acquaint your baby with different textures of materials. Touch his hand with a rattle, soft toy or pieces of cloth. He'll grasp and hold them. Objects placed in his hand should be selected carefully to avoid accidental injury. This exercise has little educational value, but it can be enjoyable for your child and others. It strengthens the family bond.

A newborn waves his hands back and forth in front of his eyes without knowing that his hands exist. A small baby has no awareness that these rapidly moving objects are a part of his own body. During the following months, he will suddenly discover his hands and spend time carefully examining them. This action is important because it is the beginning of *conscious learning activity.* With discovery of his hands, your child begins to learn about the world and about himself.

Social Development

Your baby's social relationships are influenced by several factors during the first two months. The infant who sleeps most of the time develops fewer social relationships

than the child who stays awake longer. *All babies need social contact with other people.* One of your first challenges is to discover the kinds of communication and social activities you and your child can share.

ATTRACTED BY VOICES

At this age infants have not yet made the connection between what they see and what they hear. Their field of vision is limited. They don't often look in the direction of a person who is talking to them. That is why many people don't realize that infants are attracted to voices.

When you talk to your baby and he looks in the opposite direction, you may think he isn't interested. Watch the motions made by his arms while you talk. You'll see how carefully he pays attention to the sounds you make. His arm waving may seem like a random motion without meaning. When you speak, however, his arm and hand motions keep time with the sound. The human voice is important to your infant. Listening and reacting to sound are important to his social training.

COMMUNICATION

Babies first communicate by crying. Soon your baby will begin to make different kinds of sounds, such as cooing. Most vocalizing is still in the form of crying. Careful attention to his sounds will help you interpret what your baby is trying to say.

One enjoyable social activity is to hold your baby closely and gaze into his eyes. During the first few months, your baby's eyes will brighten and his mouth will shape into his first social action: a *smile.* This is an exciting event for you. But your baby is not really smiling at you as an individual. He's smiling at a human face.

Language

When a baby is born, his five senses are usually in complete working order. He does not have

For crying out loud, can't a kid have some peace and quiet? Older siblings may show little patience when younger infants are crying. As a parent you must recognize that crying is your baby's way of coping with new experiences. He's telling you he needs something. Crying is his only way of letting you know he's hungry, afraid, in pain or in need of close physical contact.

to learn how to see, hear, smell, taste or touch. What he does require is experience. He faces new sensations for which he has no explanation. You can easily understand his confusion and difficulty.

Your baby's crying is his way of coping with these new experiences. Sometimes you may wish your child never cried at all. Crying is his only way of letting you know he has a need. Sometimes that need is very simple and easily understood. Sometimes it isn't. Because your baby cannot tell you his reason for crying, his sounds can be disturbing.

WHY DOES YOUR BABY CRY?

Soon you'll learn to understand the meaning of various cries.

Hunger—Hunger is the most frequent reason for crying. The hunger cry is often the most distinctive sound and the easiest to recognize. If you nurse your baby, you may find that your body im-

mediately prepares for nursing on hearing his call for food.

Fear—Many babies are easily frightened by loud, sudden noises, bright lights or being handled too actively. Some children enjoy being bounced or patted. Others are frightened by this. Your infant's cry of fear is usually so distinctive that you'll recognize it quickly.

Pain—Pain will almost always cause crying. Some babies are sensitive to variations in room temperature, bath water or washcloth. Some feel pain when clothing is removed or when they are not wrapped tightly in blankets.

Need for Physical Contact—The most frustrating cause of infant crying is when the baby wants close physical contact. Your baby may need frequent body contact. It's not an unreasonable demand. Some infants feel isolated and uncomfortable when separated from their mother's body by birth. Im-

agine what life in the womb is like: The baby is surrounded by warmth. As Mother moves, the baby feels rhythms and sensations. No wonder newborns want physical contact and tender handling. Rocking chairs are excellent for mothers and babies because of the rhythm.

Your baby's cries are the beginnings of his language. Your written descriptions of his sounds will help you and the family understand him better.

OTHER WORDS

Your infant will make other sounds in addition to crying. Eventually he'll babble. He'll learn to make a sound, then repeat it. During the first months, the sounds your child makes will seem almost accidental. These are part of the beginning of language. It will be fun and helpful for you to make a list of these different *words* to compare with future lists. You'll be surprised how his

How you handle your baby may determine how he reacts to you. The baby above is being handled gently by his sister. Rougher handling might have resulted in a Moro reflex response. That is when a child arches his back and throws his head backward. His arms and legs are flung upward. Such a response indicates the baby is being handled too roughly.

vocabulary changes during the first 30 months. These lists will tell you how your baby communicates with his new world.

Emotions

Your baby's emotional responses, like other functions, are not well developed. Parts of his nervous system function, but a newborn still lacks experience in dealing with life. You can expect your child to be emotional during the first two months.

Babies can have rapid emotional shifts. An infant can be crying broken-heartedly one moment and making contented sounds the next. Your infant experiences life differently than you do. A great deal of patience is required while the newborn learns to deal with ordinary problems, particularly during the first two months.

MORO REFLEX

Several emotional responses occur over which the child has no control. We mentioned the grasping reflexes of the hands and feet. Another is called the *Moro reflex*.

A baby who is handled roughly wants to cling closely to another person. A sudden change in position often produces a violent and distressing action. The baby arches his back and throws his head back. At the same time, his arms and legs fling upward, then rapidly close to the center of the body. This reflex is often accompanied by vigorous crying. The Moro reflex has no apparent function. It disappears within a relatively short time. If you observe it, you will know your handling was too vigorous and frightening for your child.

STARTLE REFLEX

Another reflex is called the *startle reflex*. This behavior is a jerking or twitching of arms and hands. It is often accompanied by a cry of fright. This may occur when the baby is startled by a sound, sees a bright light or feels a sudden change in body temperature. It can occur during changing clothes or bathing. Startles can also appear without warning during sleep. There may be no sound or other cause that you can recognize, yet the baby suddenly jumps and cries. If your baby remains asleep, there's nothing much for you to do. If startle reflexes occur while the baby is awake, do what comes naturally: stroke, cuddle and soothe him.

Emotional reflexes are a normal and natural part of infant behavior. Don't be concerned by them. Recognize that your child is experiencing life for the first time. By understanding this you will deal better with the emotional responses of your baby's early months.

Motor Development

Motor development describes your child's use of large muscles in his arms, legs and back. During the first two months, these muscles are still controlled by reflexes.

If you hold your baby under his arms in a standing position, he will appear to be walking. Place him on his stomach and a kind of scooting-crawling-swimming action occurs. This actually can move him across the crib. When placed on his back so his feet touch the side of the crib, he may arch his back and scoot across the sheets.

Babies lie in the *tonic neck reflex* position during the first several months. When a baby's head is turned to one side, the arm and leg on that side are extended. The other arm and leg are bent. If his head turns to the other side, the arms and legs reverse position. This reflex will soon disappear.

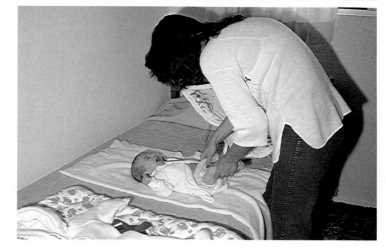

You may think your baby can't move around much during his early development. But young infants have a way of surprising you! *Never* leave your baby alone in any position from which he might fall and be injured. A quick muscle reflex may cause him to flop over when you least expect it.

As the baby grows, reflexes will disappear and be replaced by conscious activities. But reflexes are not entirely useless. They provide an involuntary exercise of the muscles. This happens before your child is old enough to use his muscles consciously.

TONIC NECK REFLEX

During his first few months, your baby will lie in what is called the *tonic neck reflex* position. When placed on his back, your baby lays his head to one side, with arm and leg on that side *extended*. The other arm and leg are slightly *bent*. When his head is turned so that it lies on the other cheek, the extended leg and arm bend. The bent leg and arm extend. In other words, as his head is turned his arms and legs reverse position.

Your baby has no control over this reflex position. His hands are always too far away from his eyes to be in focus. Only one hand is ever in direct view of his face.

All of these reflexes occur when they are triggered by circumstances over which the child has no control. Reflex activity gives your baby exercise and relief from the boredom of the crib.

PREVENT FALLS!

Reflex actions can occur suddenly and vigorously. *Even the smallest infant should never be left in any position from which a fall can occur.* Your baby can quickly arch his back, dig in his heels and scoot right off a diaper-changing table or other surface. A startle reflex may cause your baby to jump and turn over quickly.

Physical development occurs in sudden spurts. *A quiet infant who has never turned over unaided can accomplish this difficult activity suddenly.* Dangerous falls can occur without warning.

Father's Role

Today many fathers are playing primary roles in their children's lives. Some help their wives in the delivery room and share the parenting functions at home. It is no longer considered unmasculine for a father to be loving, tender and gentle with babies and toddlers.

There is a working mother in about *half* of today's young families. In such families the father may share *primary* responsibility for changing diapers, feeding, taking trips and entertaining the baby.

There is no reason fathers can't do all the child care tasks that a mother does. Father is equally responsible for the life of the baby. He can share in the great satisfaction of parenthood as the baby develops.

Your child will learn to recognize father at about the same time he recognizes mother. The relationship between father and child can deepen through the months into a loving relationship.

Your baby will find that it is more fun to have two parents instead of one. It makes life more interesting. Mother may tire at the end of the day. Then comes another person to give baby attention and play with him. Father is also interesting because he *looks* different from mother. The hair on his body is different. The way he dresses is

Fathers have an important role in child-rearing. Society no longer makes the same distinctions it once did about mothers' and fathers' duties. Father's tenderness, understanding and attention can become special factors in your child's life.

different. The way he walks and talks is different. His touch is different.

As your baby becomes a toddler there is something else he'll notice about mother and father. When he tests you to see what he can get away with, he finds that mother and father react differently. You may both say, "No, you can't do that," but you each do it differently. Your child will learn an early lesson about adults: *They not only look different, they behave differently, too.*

There will come a time in your child's development when he will decide that he really wants to please both parents. He'll study you to learn how. Each parent is important to him as he learns to interact with adults.

Diary
Months 1 & 2

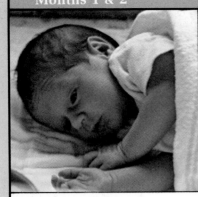

Use these diary pages to record significant events and developments in your baby's growth or behavior. These records can be useful in understanding your baby as he matures. They'll also be fun to re-read months or even years later. Get to know your baby!

Month 1:

Diary

Month 2:

About Your Child
Months 1 & 2

"Bonding" is the emotional attachment between parent and child. It is established through close physical contact. Describe behavior that suggests your baby is developing a bond with you and the family:

Your baby is unique, a real "original." What personality characteristics has he shown during the first two months that mark his individuality?

Personal schedule is important to your baby. List below the times of day he is

Hungry:

Awake:

Asleep:

Crying:

Check the behaviors listed below that best describe your baby.

Behavior	Week 1	Week 2	Week 3	Week 4	2nd Month
Wakeful					
Sleepy					
Happy					
Smiles frequently					
Irritable					
Easily frightened					
Active					
Quiet					
Heavy eater					
Light eater					

Mouth and Eyes
Months 1 & 2

The sucking reflex is a learning exercise for your baby. Describe his behavior during sucking. Is he vigorous or listless? Other characteristics?

Month 1	Month 2

Your baby is nearsighted in the first two months. He can see well in an 8- to 10-inch field of vision. He'll probably have definite preferences about what he wants to look at. In the spaces below, list objects your baby likes to look at.

Month 1	Month 2

Infants are fascinated by the human face or anything that resembles a face. They will often stare intensely at a face image. Show your baby the face on page 10 or a similar one. Describe his reaction here:

Manipulation
Months 1 & 2

Arm and hand actions are almost totally controlled by reflexes during the first two months. List below some of your child's hand activities.

Month 1	Month 2

Social Development

Your baby needs social contact with people. What kind of social behavior has he exhibited towards others in the first two months?

How does your baby respond to the voices of those listed below?

Mother's voice:

Father's voice:

Brother's or sister's voices:

Others' voices:

Language
Months 1 & 2

Crying is one of the first forms of communication. You can learn to interpret the meaning of your baby's various cries. Describe his cries of

Hunger:

Fatigue:

Fear:

Pain:

Boredom:

Loneliness (need for physical contact):

Emotions

Your baby's emotional responses are often expressed by reflexes over which he has no control. In the spaces below, describe what you've seen of

The Moro reflex (see page 12):

The startle reflex (see page 12):

Describe your baby's behavior after he experienced the Moro or startle reflex. What kind of comforting did he respond to?

Motor Development
Months 1 & 2

Motor development consists largely of reflex movements during the first two months. Describe below your child's motor abilities.

On his back:

On his stomach:

Held in a standing position:

When you play with your baby you are helping him develop motor skills. Describe how he reacts to playtime. What games does he enjoy most?

At the end of month 2, read through what you've recorded in the learning charts. Think about the progress you and your child have made. How are things going? Is his development proceeding smoothly? Use the chart below to check your progress and plan how you can guide your child in the coming months.

Area of development	Progressing very well	Could be doing better	Use the spaces below to plan what you can do to assist your child's growth and development in the areas indicated.
	Check one		
Personality			
Use of mouth and eyes			
Use of fingers and hands			
Relationships with others			
Language (crying)			
Emotions			
Ability to move around			

Months 3 & 4

Baby Talk

I have some good news for you. During the next few months, I'll be a lot easier to live with. If I made life a little exhausting for you during my first two months, I apologize. The first two months were hard for me, too.

I've learned a lot since I was born. Life isn't so unpredictable now. I'm learning that my needs for food, comfort and attention will be met. I used to feel frantic when I had a need and it wasn't met immediately. In two months I've learned to wait for someone to take care of me. Now, I'm learning to tell you what I want by different sounds and actions that I make. I'm also learning patience if you don't come running immediately.

Guess what else I've learned? I can recognize some faces and sounds. And I'm learning to control my hands. Now I can hold them in front of my eyes and carefully examine them. I can reach and grasp. Oh yes, I've also learned that a smile is a great way to get your attention!

Now that I'm awake longer during the day, I'm becoming more interested in everything around me. I see more clearly. I still can't see objects very far away, but my eyes certainly work better than they did when I was born. Now the world isn't so boring.

I'm really fascinated by what I see happening around me. But there's one little problem: I can't move around by myself. Everything still must be brought to me. I'm trapped wherever I'm put. Please make my playpen and crib as interesting as possible. I like to look around and touch things, but I can't unless you bring them to me.

My third and fourth months will probably be two of the best we'll share. Right now, I'm easy to please. I hope we can enjoy this time together!

Your baby's smiles, alertness, better vision and sense of security will make these months less stressful for you.

Looking Ahead

Your baby's first two months were probably demanding and difficult. The third and fourth months usually provide welcome relief. You and your baby began life together exhausted from the rigors of birth. You were responsible for answering her needs right away, even before you recovered your strength. For most families the first two months can be frustrating and exhausting, although some infants quickly establish routines.

The first two months of parenthood were hectic. Months 3 & 4 will probably be easier and more enjoyable.

By the third month, your baby probably will settle into predictable eating and sleeping patterns. Many children sleep through the night. Most of the feeding and digestive problems of early infancy will be solved. Generally, the baby begins to feel better about life.

THE SOCIAL SMILE

Perhaps the most enjoyable event during the third month is your baby's discovery of her *social smile*. This smile is partly a result of her developing eyesight and memory. Most infants start smiling during the third month. Others may start earlier.

There is no mistaking this special smile. Your baby will recognize a familiar face and respond with a smile that involves her whole body. Her eyes will light up and her mouth will curl into a wide grin. Even her waving arms and legs become part of the act. Her delight in recognizing you is adorable and irresistible. The smile helps to deepen the bond between your baby and you. The frequency of these smiles helps make these two months enjoyable for everyone.

SPECIAL RELATIONSHIP

Your baby will develop a special relationship with the person who feeds and cares for her. If you are breast-feeding, a close bond will develop between you and your baby. The warmth of your body feels good. Your baby has learned

Development of the *social smile* is a pleasant event for you and your baby. It usually occurs during the third month. It is called *social* because your baby will respond with such a smile when familiar faces are around.

Your baby will have two special requirements that you must fulfill during the third and fourth months: dependability and opportunity for experiences.

to depend on that warmth and comfort. She spends considerable time looking into your eyes. You are getting to know each other at a very personal level.

If your baby is bottle fed, you may be tempted to prop the bottle with a pillow and let her feed by herself. You will miss an important opportunity to enjoy a special relationship if you follow this practice. It is worth mother's or father's time to put all aside at feeding time to deepen the parent-child relationship.

A healthy and active baby laughs and smiles. This helps you feel good about your new venture into parenthood. A passive child who sleeps a lot or has health difficulties, may not smile as much. Parents often feel guilty or discouraged if their child is not sociable and smiling. Be aware that differences in temperament and behavior exist among normal infants.

Your most important function in these early months is to pay close attention to your own child. Learn what you can expect from her and what she needs from you.

CAUSE AND EFFECT

Your 3- or 4-month-old child will begin to learn the meaning of *cause and effect.* She will learn that you will respond when she gets hungry and begins to cry. She will also recognize faces and actions.

As your child begins moving her hands and feet, she will learn that a toy will move when her hand hits it. These learning experiences may not excite you, but they are adventures for your baby.

During this period, your baby begins to have some control over her own behavior. She may have just enough control to create problems. For example, a baby cries when she is hungry. Then she may become upset because of the crying and be unable to eat. She may scoot across her sheets and become wedged in the corner of the crib, unable to move. Then she cries out of frustration.

Protect your child against too much stimulation. Quick response to her hunger, pain and boredom is important.

SPECIAL NEEDS

Here are some of your baby's special needs during months 3 & 4:

Dependability—Dependable and reliable response from you becomes important as your baby begins learning from experience. Hunger cries are often quieted simply by the sound of your approach. Your baby has learned what to expect. Anticipation is an important part of her learning. You can see why reliable and predictable actions on your part are important. Your baby will have difficulty making sense of what's going on around her if your responses aren't predictable.

Opportunity—Your child must be allowed to experience things in order to learn. If she's kept in her bed or playpen with white sheets and bare walls, there's nothing visual to capture her attention. Occasionally she needs your companionship so she can smile and get smiles in return. It's important social training. Your baby's muscles can't develop rapidly unless she can be in different positions. She's a rapid learner with tremendous curiosity at this age. She needs your help in order to learn and develop.

At 3 to 4 months, your child is just about *perfect.* Most of the initial problems of life are being solved. She doesn't have to face the difficulties that come when she starts crawling and walking. This is the time when she's most beautiful, exciting, endearing and lovable. Make the most of it. Relax. Enjoy your baby!

26

About Your Child

Your baby's activities can be described in one word during the third and fourth months: *exploration.* Her uncontrollable reflexes will be replaced by conscious and voluntary actions. Her increasing neck muscle strength allows her to lie on her back and see both hands and feet. The distance increases at which her eyes can focus. It changes from 8 to 10 inches for a newborn to almost complete visual development by the end of the fourth month. These developments help your baby take a greater interest in the world.

CURIOSITY

Now your baby's curiosity will be more evident. She'll show it by her interest in your face. She may stare at you for long periods. Sometimes she may excitedly swat her hand at your face or eyes.

Her hands are involved as her curiosity develops. The reflex begins to disappear that caused your baby to clench her fists. She's able to open, close and intertwine her fingers. She discovers that those fingers belong to her and are part of her body.

MAKING CHOICES

Conscious choices and purposeful activity are evidence of your baby's mental growth. When she can see an object, she'll decide if it's interesting enough to reach for, grasp and place in her mouth. This may seem like a minor accomplishment to anyone else. For your baby this is joining several independent actions into one smooth, coordinated activity. It's not just a simple reflex. It's a series of choices, decisions and actions that your baby has made all by herself.

More of these decisions will come. These developments are an exciting part of your child's personality. They should be recognized and appreciated.

Exploration and curiosity will occupy your baby during this period. She is developing the basic ability to make choices, decisions and take actions on her own. These activities are important steps toward further development. Make sure your baby is well supported if you place her in a swing or chair during months 3 & 4. Her muscles are still developing. You must ensure that she does not fall.

PERSONALITY CLASHES AHEAD?

Personality traits make your child unique. They can become a source of problems between you and your child. A calm, quiet parent may have difficulty with an active, aggressive, demanding baby. On the other hand, an active parent may enjoy vigorous physical handling of the baby. The parent may be upset with a child who prefers a calm environment.

You may find it hard to understand all your baby's requirements. Her fussiness and crying can upset you sometimes. But you must respond to every need that you recognize. By doing so, you will make these months happier for your baby. They will also be better for you. Remember, you can't spoil your child by giving her what she must have at this age.

The 4-month-old above illustrates how the mouth is used to explore and learn about objects in her environment. She can look intensely at nearby objects. At 4 months a child's vision is actually better at close distances than an adult's. This is primarily because the child's eyes are closer together.

Mouth and Eyes

In her first two months, your baby's mouth was used for sucking and for taking food. By the third month, it has taken on new functions: exploration and learning. Your baby is developing the skill to grasp objects and place them in her mouth.

LEARNING TOOL

Your newborn had no awareness of her own body as she sucked a finger or thumb. Now this realization is coming. Her mouth is not only a place to take food but an important learning tool!

Her gumming of everything is not merely to help new teeth come through the gums, but to aid in learning.

SOLID FOOD

Your baby may be first introduced to solid food during the third and fourth months. Sucking and swallowing are reflex actions in nursing and bottle feeding that your child does not have to learn. But conscious swallowing of solid food is a different matter. It doesn't come automatically. It must be learned. If your child has difficulty learning to swallow, be patient and she'll soon catch on.

REPERTOIRE OF SOUNDS

Your baby may make gurgling sounds after eating and throaty, whimpering sounds when upset. At first, these are made without conscious effort. They are simply responses of your baby's body to her emotions. Her vocabulary of sounds increases as she listens to her own voice and yours. Your baby may begin to imitate the cough or tongue click she hears someone else making. Don't be surprised when your baby *invents* the game of coughing at you! She's learning that her mouth can be used to *communicate*.

EXPANDING VISUAL ABILITY

Eye development is rapid during the third and fourth months. At 3 months, your child still has fairly limited vision. By the end of the fourth month, her vision will be almost completely developed. When she's 4 months old she'll see better at short distances than you do because her eyes are closer together. At that age, holding a toy 3 or 4 inches away from her eyes isn't necessarily a sign of eye problems.

CONNECTING SIGHT AND SOUND

Your baby will learn to connect sounds with sights. Unlike a new-

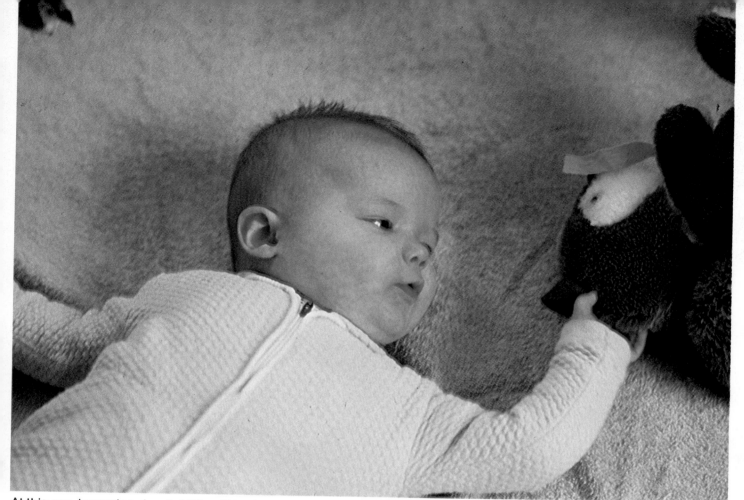

At this age, improving visual ability will lead your child to what are called *fascination objects*. These are objects that have special appeal to your baby. She may wave her hands and arms with excitement when she sees one. This 3-month-old has taken an interest in a stuffed animal. Preoccupation with such objects may momentarily draw your child's attention away from eating.

born who stares blankly into space, your baby will begin to look around when she hears a sound. She is searching for the source. She consciously decides to turn and look now that she's developing control over head movement.

Her visual skills also develop because she is able to look at objects from different angles. As neck muscles improve and she can hold up her head, your baby can be placed in a supported seated position. This will give her a better view of her surroundings.

VISUAL ATTRACTIONS

Many objects will visually attract your baby at this age. These are called *fascination objects*. When your baby sees one, she becomes excited. She may wave her hands and feet vigorously. Experiment and keep a record of these objects on page 36. Slowly move a rattle, shiny ball, colored block or even a cup across your baby's field of vision. You'll know when she's fascinated by her excited waving and kicking.

These visual attractions may interrupt your baby's other activities, such as eating. When this happens, she may do what is called *place-holding*. She stops what she is doing to stare at an object. She holds herself in readiness to continue the activity that has been interrupted. When her fascination has been satisfied, she'll resume.

Place-holding is an intentional act that teaches your baby to deal simultaneously with more than one activity. Observe her place-holding and you'll learn about her visual preferences and objects that fascinate her.

DEPTH PERCEPTION

In months 3 & 4, your baby begins to perceive and judge *depth* as she reaches for objects. Provide her with safe objects that she can see and reach to help her develop depth perception. A toy, such as an unbreakable mirror in a plastic or rubber ring, enables her to see, reach, touch and explore with her mouth. Objects hung on strings or cords are frustrating at this age. They are too difficult for her to grasp because they swing away when touched.

Manipulation

Your baby has already become fascinated with her hands and fingers. This may lead her to stare at her hands as long as 10 minutes at a time! Touching hand to hand and intertwining fingers indicate

29

she is becoming more aware of herself.

PHYSICAL PROGRESS

Hand discovery takes place because your child has progressed in several important areas. She can now lie on her back with her head straight up. She is not confined to the *tonic neck reflex* position, in which her eyes look toward one side or the other as we discussed on page 13. The grasp reflex is diminishing and her fingers are not always tightly clenched. They can be flexed and moved freely. Your baby's eyes have developed so that movement of hands and fingers can be clearly seen.

Now your baby's hands are busy. Show her a bright or interesting toy and she'll wave her arms with excitement in the direction of the object. This arm waving quickly develops into a batting or swiping motion. Within a few weeks she'll be reaching directly for the toy. Her reaching may be clumsy until she masters depth-perception.

Your baby will continue this activity until about 4 months of age. Then she'll put these skills together. She'll see an object, reach for it, grasp it and shift it from one hand to the other.

EYE-HAND COORDINATION

You can assist your child in developing skills of reaching, grasping and eye-hand coordination. Hand objects to her, but remember safety. She can injure herself with a sharp object by vigorous arm waving.

You can also construct toys for her bed or playpen to give her practice in reaching and grasping. Remember that your baby's coordination is still undeveloped. Don't hang things on a string. Attach them to a soft, flexible piece of plastic or rubber so they'll be easier to grasp.

SECURITY OBJECTS

During this period your baby may become strongly attached to a toy, blanket, hard plastic ring or particular piece of clothing. This special object will be important to your child and will be the source of endless hours of handling.

Touch and feel caused your baby to become interested in the object. In coming months, it may become a *security blanket* or love-object. Your child may want it as a continuous companion. A security blanket can actually be any object. Removing it for brief periods, even for washing, may cause problems. Wait until your baby is asleep before you launder her security blanket.

The mental attachment your child has for certain objects helps her make the transition from dependence on you to independence. It shows early resourcefulness and resilience.

Social Development

Your baby should be a social delight during her third and fourth months. Most babies are more enjoyable during this period than at any other time. Longer waking hours and declining adjustment problems will increase your child's interest in you and everything around her. In general, months 3 & 4 will be a happy time in your child's life.

Your baby will show you how she loves life. She'll smile, wave her arms, make sounds and respond to being touched and held closely.

TIME TO SOCIALIZE

It's easy to overlook an important point regarding body contact with your child. Some parents hold and rock their baby only when she's fussy and crying. She certainly should be attended to immediately when unhappy. But these should not be the only times you talk to, touch and play with her.

An important time to socialize with your baby is during her happy and contented periods.

QUIET MEALTIMES

Mealtime is an event that your child is likely to regard as a social period. You should make it a

A toy, blanket or certain piece of clothing may take on great meaning and importance to your child as a *security object.* The first attraction may be how the object feels. Later your child may want it as a constant *companion.* This attachment actually helps your child make the transition from depending on you for everything to more independence. Holding your baby in your arms while feeding is better than propping up the bottle.

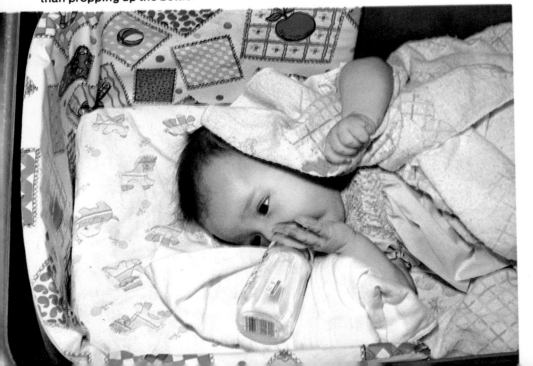

happy time. If she has other intense social times, you may need to make mealtime quieter so your baby can eat the proper amount of food.

STRANGERS ARE FRIGHTENING

Strange new faces can intimidate your baby during this period when her visual and social skills are increasing. She knows you and other family members. You can help her adjust socially to new persons by introducing them slowly and calmly. Let her become accustomed to them. Don't be surprised if your baby screams with terror when a stranger rushes in and lifts her from the crib. It can happen even if that stranger happens to be grandmother!

Language

Your baby's communication during months 3 & 4 will develop beyond cries for food or comfort. The more you learn to understand and respond to her sounds, the less she will cry.

Other sounds will develop that indicate she is happy and playful. All are the beginning of language. Your response to sounds will help your baby learn that she does not always have to cry to get attention.

BABBLING AND COOING

During the third month, most babies begin making sounds that are called *babbling*. Your baby may make a constant stream of sounds at objects and persons she sees. She may also babble while you change her diaper, bathe her or just play with her. Sometimes her chatter continues throughout her waking day.

By the end of month 3 or sometime during the fourth month, your baby may begin making *open-vowel* sounds called *cooing*. The name is an accurate one, for the sounds are much like the cooing of a dove. These vowel sounds are usually "Aaah," "Oooo" and "Oouh."

"MAMA" AND "DADA"

Consonants are added to your baby's vocabulary after a time of practicing vowels. These include B, P and M. By combining these with the vowels, your baby may form simple words like "mama," "dada," "baba" and "bye-bye."

The word-like sound that you may recognize first is "maaa." Mothers are delighted to hear this, but fathers may be upset because the baby does not yet say "daaa." This difference in language development has nothing to do with parental preference. It is because the consonant sound M is usually learned earlier than the sound D, which is more difficult to make.

Language involves more than words and sounds. Your baby tells you more about wants, needs and feelings by her behavior than by sounds. Pay close attention to her activities and sounds. Learn to respond to her infant language. It's one of the most enjoyable and interesting parts of parenthood.

Emotions

Certain characteristics begin to develop in your baby at this age. The emotional system of a 3-month-old is somewhat disorganized and unpredictable. First and most enjoyable is the expression of delight.

DELIGHT

Your child's social smile expresses her enjoyment of contact with other people. Even at this age, your baby is able to make important distinctions between different levels of delight. She smiles at enjoyable experiences and laughs at exciting events. She squeals with joy at other things.

During months 3 & 4, emotional expressions of delight will probably be a big part of your baby's personality.

FEAR

Fear will be apparent in your baby. You can predict it more easily at this age. She still has a fear of falling and fear of sudden

Your baby may enjoy social contacts during months 3 & 4. This child is delighted at being held and talked to.

bright lights or loud noises. How she expresses it is likely to be determined more by her general mood than by the particular event.

Swinging your baby in the air may bring squeals of delight when she is in a playful mood. It may bring howls of fear if she is tired or upset. The same emotional reactions may occur in response to noises and lights.

RAGE

Your baby may express rage when she becomes frustrated and loses control of herself. Most of her emotional experiences during these months are positive. You should recognize that her rage is not anger but an uncontrolled reaction to a particular frustration.

You won't spoil your baby if

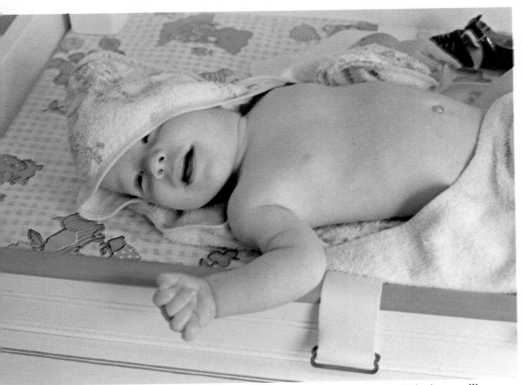

Muscle development is rapid during these months. Your baby's legs will grow stronger. This presents new dangers because of increased mobility. Be alert when your baby is on the diaper-changing table or any other high surface. One kick and she can slip over the edge.

you pay attention to this kind of uncontrolled behavior. Her intention is not to dominate or to demand but simply to have a need met. When rage occurs, it is a signal to you that your child has lost control of a situation. She needs your help.

Motor Development

The word *motor,* as used here, means the ability to control and use the large muscles—sometimes called *motor muscles.* With this ability, the child can use her arms and legs, learn to crawl and learn to walk.

Development of your baby's motor skills during months 3 & 4 is important. It leads to other learning experiences. Your child will not develop in a neat step-by-step pattern. Developing one motor skill may bring hundreds of other learning experiences within her reach.

MIDLINE POSITION

An example of expanded learning is your baby's ability to lie on her back with head, hands and feet in line with her body. During her first weeks, your baby kept her head to one side. Arms and legs were either extended or bent in the tonic neck reflex position.

During the third month, her neck muscles begin to strengthen. Your baby will be able to lie on her back and *look straight ahead* in the *midline position.* Both arms and legs will be bent with the legs slightly raised. In this position, your baby can voluntarily move her head back and forth and freely move her arms and legs. The important gain is her ability to hold her hands in front of her face and examine them. This development of motor ability and free movement of her hands open many other learning opportunities.

RAISED HEAD

Improvement of neck muscles allows your baby to hold her head up in a near-vertical position when she is on her stomach. This allows her to look around. She can exercise her increasing visual ability and become acquainted with her surroundings. She is also able to look up and search for you when she hears you coming.

LEG STRENGTH

Leg exercise is possible when your baby is on her back. She'll have surprising leg strength by the end of her fourth month. She'll be able to move her entire body with her legs when her feet touch the side of the crib or playpen.

DANGER FROM MOBILITY

A danger of rapid development is that your baby may become much stronger and more mobile than you realize. Suddenly without warning, she'll be scooting and rolling all over the place. You should take great care not to leave your baby, even for a moment, in a place where she can fall.

PLAYPEN TRAINING GROUND

Carefully consider your baby's time in her playpen. Restrictions of a playpen will be very frustrating after she has learned to crawl. But during months 3 & 4 while she is developing scooting and turning abilities, the playpen is an *enjoyable* and *safe* place. It provides her with new and different visual experiences within well-controlled boundaries.

If you intend to use a playpen with your child, you should begin during months 3 & 4.

The Working Mother

Some mothers of very young infants must work outside the home to make ends meet. Other mothers put off returning to work for the first three years of their children's lives. Much has been said, both pro and con, about the effect on infants of being away from their working mothers.

Recent research indicates that children even as young as 2 months are not harmed by good day care. Yet some working mothers may feel cheated because they miss so much of their child's babyhood.

Babies do not choose parents. Very young babies can be satisfied with substitute parents during the workday. The arrangement works as long as the substitutes are loving and meet the babies' needs. Babies don't know the difference between parents and substitutes. However, they gradually begin to look forward to the arrival of parents from work. Parents become two more interesting adults who give attention and love.

SPEND QUALITY TIME

Your baby can form bonds with substitute parents as well as with you. The *quality*, not the *quantity*, of time you spend with your baby is the important factor. Your child does not understand that as a working parent you are probably tired after work. She will still want attention, to be played with, voices to listen to and lots of cuddling.

Perhaps the worst time to start work is when your baby is 9 to 16 months old. That's when *bonding*, described on page 7, becomes a deep attachment. Your baby must learn to trust you and know you will return when you leave her. Until then

When a mother works outside the home, good day care for the baby is very important. Day care centers or baby sitters should be reliable, trustworthy and loving. If you work, or intend to, it is best to visit the center or individual with your child. Make sure that your child will be properly cared for.

she may be fearful that you have deserted her completely. No substitute can take your place in this situation.

DAY CARE

There are certain things to look for if you decide to go to work and must hire a baby sitter or use a day care center. The most important qualities are the reliability, qualifications and trustworthiness of the adult whom you hire. He or she must sincerely love children and be able to meet your baby's needs. One adult can't meet the needs of more than *two infants*. But an adult can handle three or four *older* youngsters.

Your child will enjoy arrangements where the people she sees are there every day. Some centers are manned by volunteers. Helpers are con-

stantly changing. This is difficult for children who need one person to count on.

Choose a baby-sitting plan where there is a mixture of routine and freedom. Visit the center or home several times with your child. Be sure your baby will be well cared for. These visits will also help prepare your child for the coming changes in her life.

When a child reaches 2 years old, she will be interested in other children. By the time she is 3, she can really enjoy group play. The change comes gradually and can't be rushed. Your child may be on guard with other children and do no more than watch for several months. If all goes well, she'll eventually relax and begin to join in the fun. She'll benefit from group play and become more sociable.

Diary

Months 3 & 4

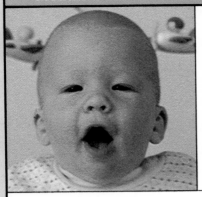

Use these diary pages to record significant events and developments in your baby's growth or behavior. These records can be useful in understanding your baby as she matures. They'll also be fun to re-read months or even years later. Get to know your baby!

Month 3:

34

Month 4:

About Your Child

Body exploration will play a role in your baby's developing personality during months 3 & 4. Describe your child's activities in exploring her hands and feet:

Your baby is learning to do things purposely. List any actions that appear to be consciously initiated by your baby:

Mouth and Eyes

Your baby's skills using mouth and eyes will increase during these months. Describe below what your child can do.

During month 3	During month 4
With mouth:	With mouth:
With eyes:	With eyes:

Interest in looking at objects increases dramatically during your baby's 3rd and 4th months. What objects are especially attractive to her now? List below (see *fascination objects*, page 29):

Manipulation
Months 3 & 4

Certain toys, a blanket or a piece of clothing may take on great importance to your baby as her *security object*. She may want to hold or handle it constantly. What objects especially attract your baby this way?

How does she react when the objects are removed?

Your baby's hands will be busy during these months as her manipulation skills develop. Chart her finger and hand progress below.

Skill	Month 3			Month 4		
	Not yet adept	Fair	Excellent	Not yet adept	Fair	Excellent
Flexing fingers						
Reaching						
Grasping						
Eye-hand coordination						

Social Development
Months 3 & 4

Your child's sociability may be very high during months 3 & 4. When is she at her BEST or WORST socially? Chart her schedule below.

	Best	OK	Not so good
When she wakes up			
Breakfast			
Lunch			
Dinner			
Other mealtimes			
After a nap			
Bedtime			

Your baby may not react well to a stranger, even if it's grandmother! Describe how she behaves when a strange person pays close attention to her:

Whom does your baby recognize?

For whom will she smile?

Language
Months 3 & 4

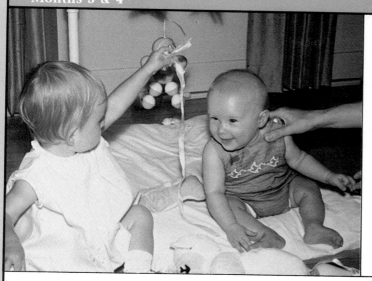

Your baby's language will develop beyond mere cries for food or comfort during months 3 & 4. Consonant and vowel sounds enable her to begin forming simple word-like sounds. Describe sounds that she can make:

What were your baby's language differences between months 3 & 4?

Sounds at month 3:

Sounds at month 4:

Language involves more than words or sounds. Describe your baby's NONVERBAL communications (for example, body movements or facial expressions) that tell you when she wants or needs something:

Emotions

Your baby's emotional system is still disorganized. She can clearly show fear or rage. List situations below that stimulate those emotions in your child.

Fear:

Rage:

A 3- or 4-month-old baby is usually happy and full of delight. Make a happiness list below.

Situations that make your baby smile:

That make her laugh:

That make her squeal with glee:

Motor Development

Your baby will spend a lot of time on her back during her first few months (see tonic neck reflex position and midline position, page 32). Later, she can lie on her stomach. Describe different behavior you've observed when your baby is in these positions.

Lying on back:

Lying on stomach:

Chart your baby's motor developments and record calendar dates when they began.

Skill	Date	Skill	Date
Kicking and thrashing		**Scooting**	
Holding head up		**Rolling over**	
Pushing with feet		**Other**	

Check Your Progress
Months 3 & 4

At the end of month 4, read through what you've recorded in the learning charts. Think about the progress you and your child have made. How are things going? Is her development proceeding smoothly? Use the chart below to check your progress and plan how you can guide your child in the coming months.

Area of development	Progressing very well	Could be doing better	Use the spaces below to plan what you can do to assist your child's growth and development in the areas indicated.
	Check one		
Personality			
Use of mouth and eyes			
Use of fingers and hands			
Relationships with others			
Language (crying, sounds)			
Emotions			
Ability to move around			

Baby Talk

Fun! That's what these last few months have been for all of us. You can see I'm not so frantic and fearful anymore.

I'm looking forward to the next few months. We can do many more things together. You must have felt like a servant until now. I just couldn't do anything for myself. I hope you understood.

I'm eating and sleeping on a more regular schedule now. That should give you time to catch up on your rest. Now we can be real friends and enjoy each other. You know what makes me feel good right now? Just the sight of your face and sound of your voice.

I admit I like a good time. It's simple to keep me happy. Here's what I like:

Playing games with you and having a good laugh.

Doing things alone, like playing with my hands.

Kicking, squirming, rolling.

Toys!

I'll begin moving around by myself before my fifth, sixth and seventh months are over.

I'll be able to sit up alone and I can watch you. I'll also know when you're not in the room. I may not like to see you leave. Please take me with you and just let me watch. After all, now I'm beginning to see everything. I like to go from place to place with you.

You've noticed how curious I am. I like to see, hear or touch everything. But I still need your guidance. Give me interesting things to explore. I need you to bring the world to me.

Some things I do may disturb you at times. I repeat things a lot, simply for practice. You must get tired of picking up toys I drop and throw. My table manners are a real mess. But I'm having fun. Please be patient for a few months. Eventually I'll learn to do things better.

Your baby's curiosity and desire to explore will increase during this period.

Looking Ahead

Months 5—7 will be a continuation of the enjoyment that began during months 3 & 4. Unless teething or illness interrupt, your baby will enjoy life during this period. You'll enjoy him, too.

FULL OF ENERGY

Your baby is changing rapidly. Your once quiet and placid child is active and energetic. This is a period of intense physical activity. Your baby may seem in perpetual

Babies are a joy during months 5—7, as the family at left shows.

motion. He's waving his arms and legs, making sounds, rolling over, kicking and scooting.

He's also awake for longer periods, mostly during the day. He may sleep through the night regularly. But his desire for physical movement may occasionally interrupt his nighttime sleep. You may hear him awaken in the night, make sounds and move around. Then he'll go back to sleep.

More waking hours combined with improving eyesight means your child is becoming more aware of surrounding objects and people. He's more excited about all his new discoveries.

MEMORY AND LEARNING

Have you noticed that your baby is developing a *memory*? This means he now has the ability to *learn from experience*. He'll be able to do more new things as his memory and experiences increase.

He's learning so rapidly that you can almost see him change daily.

This is the last time in your baby's life when you can put him someplace where he'll stay and enjoy it. Before these three months are over, he'll be moving around. He'll never again be completely under your control. Enjoy your baby because his brief infancy will soon disappear.

SOLID FOOD

Your baby will eat more solid food now that his hand and finger abilities are increasing. He can feed himself to a small extent. Clumsy attempts at feeding are made even worse because he'll make mealtime a play period. He may spit, throw, blow bubbles, dribble and generally make a terrible mess.

If there are other children in the family, his messy habits may become worse. They laugh at his antics. The importance of self-feeding and social benefits of having your baby with the family at mealtime make the disturbance worthwhile. There will be less mess when his hand coordination gets better. Until that time, put a sheet or tablecloth under his highchair or feeding table. You'll feel better about the mess. Your child will get to practice eating and being with the family.

SPECIAL NEEDS

Here are some special needs that occur during months 5—7:

Practice—Curiosity grows as your baby develops new abilities. When he discovered his hands, he stared at them and moved his fingers. He touched hand to hand and tried every combination of movement until he developed hand skills. This intense curiosity begins to increase. Your baby is fascinated by nearly everything. But he needs practice to master skills that come with physical growth. Curiosity causes him to try something over and over until it is mastered. Pay close attention to the energy your child invests in learning to turn over, scoot, crawl or walk. You'll better understand the driving force of curiosity that he is experiencing.

Your baby is frustrated when he's confined too tightly by bedclothes, crib or playpen. You can relieve his boredom and educate him without spending much money for toys and equipment.

Messiness at mealtime is almost automatic now that your child's hand and finger abilities are improving. The cleanup afterward may try your patience. Your child's self-feeding attempts are a necessary part of growth and development.

Carefully observe his interests and you can provide what he needs from items you have at home.

Companionship—Your baby will need the companionship of other people during this period. He needs playtime with others in addition to the closeness he gets from the one who feeds and cares for him. Simple social games will delight him. You may enjoy them as well because your baby is so lovable and playful. A game of peekaboo will delight you both. *Play with your baby!* Don't worry about doing the right thing. Your baby's reactions to what you do can guide you. When he becomes more mobile, he won't be as interested in playing. This social play is important to your baby. It's an enjoyment you shouldn't miss.

Protection—Your baby's mobility will probably progress to creeping, crawling or even walking during months 5—7. He'll no longer be confined to the relative safety of crib and playpen. Now he'll begin to encounter new and dangerous situations. Babies of this age are especially susceptible to injury from falls. They can pull objects onto themselves, such as free-standing bookcases. All kinds of items around the house can be swallowed, stepped on or fallen on.

Now's the time to babyproof your entire house as discussed on page 60. Go through it on your hands and knees and remove *everything* that could be dangerous to your child. Install *gates* or *childproof latches* to control access to dangerous areas. Insert *safety plugs* into unused electrical sockets. It's also wise to remove or safely relocate anything your baby could destroy or damage. Move small valuables like glass or ceramic knickknacks.

Before learning to crawl or walk, your baby may love to use a walker. It gives him the mobility to satisfy curiosity. A well-constructed, high-quality walker provides good exercise. It also makes your baby mobile very quickly. If you decide to use a walker, be careful to anticipate dangerous things he can reach or pull over. Keep an eye on him. Walkers occasionally tip over.

TIME TO EXPLORE

Curiosity, rapid physical development and increasing mobility will change your child dramatically by the end of these three months. Interesting things are no longer just those that are close at hand. He can now explore and make things happen. The relatively quiet enjoyment between you and the baby during the past months is now practically over. A new, exciting, active phase of life is about to begin.

Babyproofing your house is a must if you want to ensure your child's safety. Lamps that might tip over are a hazard for your curious youngster. Tables and vases also are potential danger.

High steps can mean nasty falls and injuries for your crawling child. One solution is to install folding gates to control your baby's access to danger zones.

About Your Child

Rapid growth and development during months 5—7 will be spectacular. You may be tempted to compare your child to others the same age. Don't take these comparisons seriously. Remember that a wide range of differences is normal among children.

During these months, your child will learn to reach and grasp easily with both hands. He'll learn to roll from side to side and turn over from back to stomach and stomach to back. He'll sit upright without being held or propped, scoot or creep along the floor, and stand up alone. Progress is different for every child. Your baby's muscle development will deter-mine his pace. You can help him by close attention and playing. *You can't rush his skill development.* Your baby knows best when his muscles are ready.

QUIET

Your baby may be quiet at this age. He may spend a lot of time looking at his hands and feet. He'll calmly hold and stare at toys, shifting them from hand to hand. He may seem to be mentally investigating everything.

ACTIVE

Some babies are physically active. Your baby may spend most of his waking hours making sounds. He may learn to sit, scoot, crawl and stand earlier than a quiet child.

There are also social differences. Your baby may be outgoing and socially energetic. Or he may be contented with his own company.

Your child's distinct preferences will become more apparent as he gains personal control over behavior. His curiosity will be intense. He'll be fascinated by virtually everything he sees, touches and hears. This fascination and curiosity will give you an opportunity for game-playing with your baby. You'll have a chance to learn about his personality.

While you are becoming acquainted, your baby's personality will develop more. His self-examination, sound-making and sound imitation continue to teach him about his own uniqueness. He's learning to communicate.

FACE IN THE MIRROR

Your baby will show great interest in himself at this age. One day he will connect his mirror image with the sounds he's making. This developmental stage has been called *the age of the mirror and me.* Recognition of his face in a mirror indicates he's becoming more aware of himself.

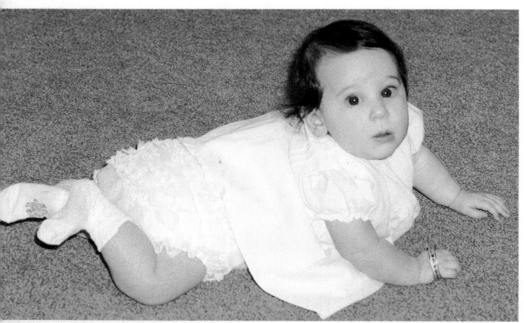

Development during the fifth, sixth and seventh months will be extensive for your baby. You can't rush skills. You should never compare your baby's development with another child. Some children are quiet types with a great interest in looking at things. These children may show intense curiosity and an early need to explore everything.

Mouth and Eyes

Your baby's eyes will replace his mouth as the primary means of learning and exploring. His mouth will be used more often for experimenting with sounds. He will also learn to eat solid foods. Learning is not very difficult as long as you are patient and recognize that the task requires practice. Don't worry about the amount of food your baby eats or how long he takes to learn this new skill.

Your baby can now see as well as or better than you. His improved vision brings with it an increased amount of interest. He can lift his head while lying on his stomach. He can inspect his new surroundings, which are now in focus. He can turn his head from side to side when he's on his back. His eyes can focus on moving objects.

VISUAL EXAMINATION

A close relationship develops between eye and hand. A few months ago your baby began reaching for objects to make them move. Then he grasped objects and put them in his mouth. Now he grasps objects to *look* at them.

Visual examination can be very intense. Your baby will hold a toy, move it from hand to hand, turn it over and stare at it.

Visually directed reaching is a technical name for an important skill that your baby will learn. His eyes direct his hands as he learns to judge distance between object and hand. *Depth perception*, visually directed reaching and *eye-hand coordination* are skills he'll learn with practice. These skills provide hours of joyful entertainment for most babies. Your baby will give these eye-hand activities serious concentration. This is an indication of their educational importance.

Expanded vision causes your baby to look around for the source of sounds, especially footsteps. You may also notice that he recognizes differences in footsteps and voices. Watch him when he hears

Dropping and throwing objects may become a favorite pastime of your child. This activity helps your child learn space perception and develop muscles. Retrieving toys may be annoying sometimes, but it's an opportunity to help your baby learn. This child has already learned to stand and drop objects from his playpen. Most children don't stand until a later age. But they will drop things from their highchair.

the one who provides his primary care and feeding. He will greet that person with distinct motions and sounds.

DROPPING AND THROWING

Your child's interest in moving things can frustrate you. Your baby will be intrigued by objects he learns to drop and throw. By the end of the seventh month, he may repeatedly drop toys from his highchair. He may throw them out of the playpen. As quickly as you

retrieve them, he'll drop or throw them again. Realize that this is his means of learning *space perception*. Don't let it annoy you.

One characteristic unique to this age is *fascination with small objects*. Your baby can see objects very close to his face. Pieces of lint, crumbs and other tiny objects become attractive. He'll pick them up, look at them and usually put them in his mouth. For that reason, be persistent in removing small objects around the house. If you don't, your baby will!

First Tooth

Your child's first tooth will appear at about 6 months. A bottom front tooth usually emerges, followed in a few weeks by another bottom front tooth. You'll notice a small pale bump for several days before the tooth actually comes through the gums.

Teething has been vastly overemphasized. Teeth that appear early cause little or no difficulty for your baby. His biting teeth are sharp and come through the gum easily. Your baby may chew on toys and dribble a lot of saliva. All you need do is wipe off the saliva and offer him hard food to chew. He may like zwieback bread, hard crusts, a piece of peeled apple or a raw carrot.

These foods serve as good early teething objects. Be certain that your baby doesn't choke on such food. A quick pat on the back between the shoulder blades will help your child cough out a piece of food from his windpipe. Later tooth development is discussed on pages 68 and 83.

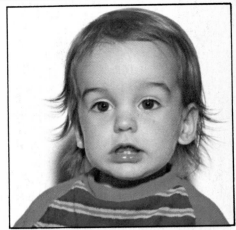

The first lower tooth usually appears at about 6 months, closely followed by a second.

Manipulation

Your baby's fists, clenched from the grasp reflex, will open to a new sensation: *touch*. Now that his fingers move independently, he'll begin to explore objects by touching them. Another development, the ability to *rotate his wrists*, adds flexibility to your baby's skills. A toy can be seen, reached for, grasped, turned over and over and explored with his fingers and eyes.

SENSORIMOTOR SKILLS

Another learning opportunity is added to your baby's skills: *listening to the sound made by toys*. He may vigorously pound an object on his highchair tray or beat two toys together. This sound is a nuisance to you. But it is his way of developing and practicing *sensorimotor skills*, the combination of sensory and motor skills. These skills join seeing, hearing and touching with the use of muscles. This is a major learning step.

APPOSING THUMB

Your baby's practice with his hands culminates in use of the *apposing thumb*. This means that his finger and thumb can be pinched together, allowing his hand to pick up and manipulate small objects. Your baby will combine this ability with his fascination for small objects. He may enjoy picking up and feeding himself small pieces of food after this skill has developed. He was able to hold and eat biscuits or crackers at a younger age. Now the ability to pick up *small* bits of food is a sign that he's completed another learning step.

Sometime during months 5—7, your baby's strengthening back

Touching things will become a major way of learning for your child. As his ability to rotate his wrists increases, he will grasp, turn over and examine toys with his hands and eyes.

muscles may allow him to sit up without support. This ability will open another new range of learning opportunities. Toys beside your seated baby can be seen, picked up, examined, dropped, retrieved and passed from hand to hand. Now *several* toys can be offered and he can choose and manipulate them at will.

VISION RANGE INCREASES

A new field of vision appears when your child learns to sit unsupported. He had approximately 180 degrees of vision when lying against a chair or infant seat. Now he can look around with a vision range of almost 360 degrees. He may sometimes lose his balance with all this head shifting. New vistas may prove so interesting that he'll practice moving into an upright sitting position. This will continue until the difficult task is mastered.

LEARNING TO RELEASE

The next skill for your baby to learn is *release*. Grasping progressed from a reflex to a consciously chosen motion. Learning to release an object has to be accomplished without help from an inborn reflex. When release is mastered, he'll be able to drop and throw. Sometimes he may drop every toy placed near him, then cry because there are no more to drop. Place them all back near him and they'll be systematically dropped again. This little game may exhaust you, but your baby will never seem to tire of it.

Dropping and throwing is a way to explore the meaning of cause and effect. Your baby's repeated dropping of toys and listening to the sounds becomes an intentional act. This process signals an important part of his education: *ability to plan and set a goal.*

HELP FROM MEMORY

Your baby's memory now allows him to relate a past event to future activities. His physical abilities also let him follow through on what his mind intends. Knowing this may relieve your frustration at constantly picking up dropped toys. You can see that it's not such a useless activity after all.

Grasping, holding, touching and throwing will excite your baby. Hand activities may become his favorite pastime. If this happens, it could mean he'll be slower than other children in learning to creep or crawl. This does not mean that creeping or crawling will never occur. They will, in due time.

Follow your baby's lead and help him with the skills he's interested in now. Creeping and crawling may be delayed by a month or two. Enjoy this time before your baby literally starts getting into everything. You'll have your hands full when creeping and crawling begin.

Social Development

Bonding between you and your child that occurred immediately after birth will now expand into a more mature relationship.

Your baby can see you, hear you, remember you and even anticipate the sight of your face. Babies of this age will often develop distinctive ways of greeting each family member. The baby's movements, smiles and sounds when mother appears may be different from the response to father.

Relationships with other people are important for your child. These two youngsters are showing an innocent affection that is part of early social training.

Curiosity and affection can combine in your baby's social training, even with the family pet!

It is important for you to make the relationship dependable and predictable. Always behave consistently when you are with your child.

His familiarity with you may lead to a desire to have you constantly in view. For a period during these months, you may have to move your baby from place to place so he can see you. This way he learns from new visual experiences. After all, his bed or playpen can become boring!

SOCIAL INTERPLAY

These are months when your baby will develop skills of social interplay. He'll be inclined to giggle and exchange smiles, laughs and sounds with others. Tickling and hugging are simple but important social games you can play with him. Peekaboo, This Little Pig Went to Market, finger play, and Where's the Baby? are games you can play. They can be fun for everyone in the family. They are an important means of establishing social relationships for your baby.

SHYNESS

By the end of month 7, your baby may become shy with strangers or persons who appear infrequently. Shyness is very evident in some babies. It develops because your baby is now able to tell one person from another. Both sight and memory have developed sufficiently so that he knows when a face is unfamiliar. Shyness is not uncommon with this increase in abilities, although your child may not go through this stage.

Teething discomfort may also add to shyness. Tooth development doesn't seem to be related to social skills, but discomfor may decrease your baby's desire to be sociable.

Contact with people teaches your child skills of social interplay. Your baby's giggling, smiling and laughing are part of this learning process. You and other members of the family can play simple games to help ensure your baby's success in social ventures.

Language

Your baby's verbal skills during months 5—7 are surprising, considering the short time he's had to develop them. The *clarity* of communication depends on how dependably you listen and respond to his sounds. Your baby can coo with pleasure and chortle with satisfaction. He can giggle while playing, squeal with excitement and laugh with delight. He can grunt in complaint, growl with frustration and howl with dissatisfaction. He can also communicate hunger, pain, fear and boredom. The seriousness of his communication is determined by volume, pitch and intensity of his sounds.

But your baby also communicates through *nonverbal behavior.* Body posture and facial expressions are other ways he can talk to you. Watch your baby's expressions and behavior. You'll be able to tell what the message is.

REPEATING SOUNDS

Your child will continue babbling during months 5—7, an activity that began in months 3 & 4. Babbling is *intentional repetition of sounds.* When your baby learns a new sound, he may repeat it many times. This process teaches him to make a sound, listen to it and repeat it exactly. If you respond to a sound he makes, he may repeat it to see if you'll respond the same way again.

His nonsense babbling varies in rhythm, pitch and intensity. It often sounds like adult conversation. Babbling lasts only a few months. Tape record some of his babbling. You'll capture an interesting part of your child's growth that otherwise will soon be lost.

LIMITED SOUND RANGE

The range of spoken sounds your baby makes is still limited. Vowel sounds are frequently heard along with some of the simple consonants such as P, B and M. He'll learn to speak these sounds in different arrangements. They begin with *single-syllable* sounds and move to repetition of more than one syllable at a time. By the end of these months, your baby may create a *three-syllable* sound. This is done by repeating single syllables.

The repetition of "ba-be-ba" may be shortened into a single word of three syllables, "abeba." Early sounds from babies are similar, but your baby will develop his own. Help family members recognize the baby's language. Keep a written record of his sounds on the chart on page 58.

READ TO YOUR BABY

You'll understand many of your child's words even before he actually speaks them correctly. That's why talking and reading to him are worthwhile activities. The whole family can help do this. Reading to your baby at this age may seem useless, but it is helpful. Sitting on your lap and listening to you read is a pleasurable way for him to hear words. Soft cloth or heavy paper books are appropriate at this age because your baby can't destroy the book while you read. Plastic laminated books can also be handled by the baby without damage.

Reading aloud can be a significant way of helping your child learn to talk. He won't understand words at first. Comprehension will come eventually. Durable books that the baby can play with and look at help develop his interest and encourage hand and finger abilities.

Crawling is a complicated maneuver for your baby to learn. Learning the skill is helped by your child's natural desire to explore, touch and grasp everything in the house.

himself by pushing with his feet on the mattress. While his leg muscles are being developed, his back and neck muscles strengthen. Then he can turn over. Even with limited development, some babies can achieve considerable locomotion in crib, playpen or on the floor. They scoot and roll. It's primitive, but it works.

Before beginning to move around, your child may learn to sit alone. Then he'll scoot with a combination of pushes from his arms and one leg, while the other leg is curled underneath. Another technique is to raise his head high while lying on his stomach. Then he propels himself in a series of lifts and collapses. The classic crawling position on hands and knees is a complicated maneuver. It is difficult to learn. Some babies crawl later than others. Some may develop another effective means of moving around without having to learn to crawl.

Curiosity gives your baby patience and persistence in learning to be mobile. He learns to move around because he's interested in reaching or touching something.

CRAWL, THEN WALK

The crawling-walking sequence varies among children. The age it is learned also varies. Your child's motivation to keep moving around is simple. It satisfies his curiosity and helps him learn.

GIVE HIM THE CHANCE

Don't be too concerned about when your child starts crawling or walking. Just provide opportunities for him to practice and master these skills. Confinement to crib or playpen doesn't provide enough chance to learn. Placing him on a blanket on the floor for a while each day is the best help you can provide.

Remember, once your baby begins moving around, every part of your house must be examined. Remove dangers to assure his safety.

Emotions

The range of emotions that your baby experienced in months 3 & 4 is still present in month 7. This is a period of rapid growth and change.

Healthy babies will be joyful and delightful during these months. Learning is exciting for your baby. His curiosity will increase. *The dominant emotional mood of these three months is joy,* but there will also be *unhappy* periods.

Your baby's curiosity makes him alert to changes occurring around him. He may be more affected by your emotional state than you realize. If you are upset, tense or unhappy, your baby may sense it and imitate your mood.

Motor Development

This phase of development marks the end of two major handicaps: *being trapped in a horizontal position* and *lack of mobility.* By the end of month 7, his muscles will be ready for upright mobility.

PRIMITIVE LOCOMOTION

Your child will be in almost constant motion during this period. He'll kick vigorously, scoot across the crib on his back and propel

Right and Wrong

Your child will have no understanding of right and wrong at first. How can he? He's an explorer in a new world trying to make sense of his environment. Adults swoop down on him when he does wrong from the adult point of view. But from his perspective, all explorations are a way to learn. What other way does he have?

GUIDE YOUR CHILD SOCIALLY

You must get to know your child well and learn to communicate. Then you can meet his needs. Your child needs to understand what is right and wrong. *It is your responsibility to guide your child to socially acceptable behavior.* He needs answers about how to survive.

It is difficult for you to know that your child needs, really *begs,* for guidance. Understand that his temper tantrums are the equivalent of pleas for help. Your child is overwhelmed by seething emotions. "Mom, I need your help. I don't know how to behave," is one meaning behind bad behavior. "Dad, stop me from doing what I don't understand" is another message delivered by tantrums.

Your child is saying, in effect, "Hey, someone, stop me from behaving badly all the time. I'm *independent,* yet I'm still so *dependent.*"

Right and wrong are defined by society. Your child can learn through you what society will accept. *You must translate right and wrong to your child by your behavior. This shows your approval or disapproval.*

Lessons on right and wrong are not learned overnight. Your child must test every situation and determine whether your reaction is approval or disap-

Understanding right from wrong is a distinction your young child can't make alone. You must guide him with your responses to what he's doing. This requires a consistent and clear show of approval or disapproval for your child to learn what you consider acceptable. It takes time, but with praise for good behavior your baby will learn.

proval. He can't know it is wrong to poke a neighbor's baby. He will know it when he has tried it and been *told* it is wrong. He can't know it is right to say "thank you" until he has tried it and been *praised.*

You must set the rules for right and wrong behavior. For each situation, you must approve and reinforce right behavior. You must ignore or voice disapproval for wrong behavior.

Right and wrong have no meaning to your child except that his behavior was approved or disapproved by mother and father. The understanding of morality in the adult sense will come eventually, but not for many years.

Situation by situation, month by month, your patient guidance is needed. Your child will gradually learn what is right and wrong.

Diary

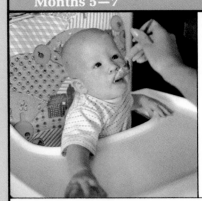

Use these diary pages to record significant events and developments in your baby's growth or behavior. These records can be useful in understanding your baby as he matures. They'll also be fun to re-read months or even years later. Get to know your baby!

Month 5:

Diary

Month 6:

Month 7:

About Your Child
Months 5—7

Mirrors and self-images will begin to fascinate your baby during this age period. Allow him to spend some time in front of a mirror and describe his reactions here:

How is your baby's personality changing during this period? Describe.

He is	Most of the time	Often	Seldom
Active			
Quiet			
Seeking attention			
Content alone			
Curious			
Messy at mealtime			

Mouth and Eyes

Your baby's first tooth may appear at about 6 months of age. However, teething progress varies among children. Your baby may not have teeth for a few more months. Describe his progress below.

When did the first tooth appear?	The second?	Have any other teeth emerged?

Your child's visually directed reaching, eye-hand coordination and space perception will improve at this age (see page 47). Record his progress below.

Activity	Record dates when these behaviors began.		
	Month 5	Month 6	Month 7
Intense visual examination of objects			
Visually directed reaching			
Good eye-hand coordination			
Interest in solid food			
Interest in small objects			

Manipulation
Months 5—7

Repeated dropping of objects from playpen or highchair develops space perception. It also develops finger, hand and arm skills. Describe your baby's interest in dropping and throwing:

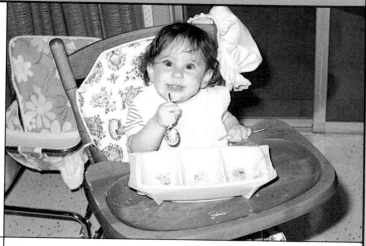

Certain objects may have special appeal to your baby for touching and feeling. What are they?

Your child may be delighted by sounds made by some objects. List the objects:

Dropping and throwing may become a favorite pastime for your baby. What objects appeal to him most for this activity?

Social Development

Personal relationships are becoming increasingly important to your child, especially with mother, father and brothers or sisters. Your baby enjoys your company. How does he get your attention?

Your baby knows his family well by this age and is aware of strangers. Describe his responses to

Mother

Father

Other family members

Strangers

Doing things with people is important for your baby. Games will delight him. Make a record below of your games.

Games baby loves:	Games he doesn't enjoy:

Language

Your child's ability to make words and sounds has probably improved. He still won't understand word meanings. Are his words clearer now? Are his words longer or more complex? List them below.

Words or sounds:	Date first heard:

Reading by any member of the family helps your child's language development. Record below his reactions to reading.

When is the best time to read to your baby?

Reaction	Morning	After lunch	Before nap	Bedtime	Other
Loves it					
Pays little attention, prefers playing					
Sits quietly and attentively					
Plays with book, seems not to listen					

Is there a special kind of book your baby seems to enjoy most?

Emotions
Months 5—7

The dominant emotional mood of months 5—7 is joy, but there are unhappy times as well. Your baby's responses to his environment are becoming clearer now. Describe what makes him happy or unhappy.

Happy	Unhappy

Your emotions are contagious. You may see your baby respond with a similar mood if you are tense or upset. Can you recall times when your emotions were transferred to your child?

Date	Times when you were unhappy or upset	Your baby's reaction

Your baby is no longer trapped horizontally, nor is he immobile. Describe how he moves about by rolling over, scooting, lifting and collapsing or pushing.

At 5 months:

At 6 months:

At 7 months:

Increasing mobility can put your child into danger zones throughout the house. Check those areas you have already babyproofed. List others that need attention.

Electrical outlets and cords		Sharp objects		Screen doors that open easily	
Poisons in kitchen, bathroom, elsewhere		All dangerous small objects		Pet food and pet dishes	
Lamps		Exposed hot water pipes		Others:	
Heaters/furnaces		Glassware, ashtrays			
Stairways		Other breakable items			
Unstable furniture that could tip		Tools or equipment			

Check Your Progress
Months 5—7

At the end of month 7, read through what you've recorded in the learning charts. Think about the progress you and your child have made. How are things going? Is his development proceeding smoothly? Use the chart below to check your progress and plan how you can guide your child in the coming months.

Area of development	Progressing very well	Could be doing better	Use the spaces below to plan what you can do to assist your child's growth and development in the areas indicated.
	Check one		
Personality			
Use of mouth and eyes			
Use of fingers and hands			
Relationships with others			
Language			
Emotions			
Ability to move around			

Baby Talk

Life's much more interesting now. I can see everything that's going on. Seeing is much easier because I can sit up. Sometimes I'm unhappy if I can't be right in the middle of everything you're doing.

I'll be trying a lot of new and exciting things during the next five months. I can already scoot around on the floor a little. Soon I'll be quicker than a wink. When my hands and knees work together properly, I'll be crawling all over the house! If I learn to crawl well, I may not have to learn to walk immediately.

I'm glad those long months of lying on my back in my crib are over. It's more fun to explore everywhere. Sometimes I don't even want to stop to eat or sleep. That's when I need your patience and guidance to make sure I get my meals and my rest on time.

Our house is a delight. I'm interested in everything I see. I like to open cabinets and pull on curtains. I chase after sounds when I hear someone moving around.

Mom, I suspect you get tired of having me with you every minute. You're very special to me. You seem to appear and disappear so easily! I'm frightened if you're not right where I left you when I return from exploring another room. That's why I always seem to be under your feet. I don't want to lose you! After a few months, I'll know that you don't really disappear just because I can't see you. But right now I'm not quite sure what happens to you. I want you close to me.

My growth is bringing some advantages, too. I don't cry as much. Now I can let you know what I want by means other than crying. We can enjoy more smiles and fewer tears because we are communicating better.

Almost everything will interest your child at this age.

I like it when you get down on the floor to play. It's fun to roll around and chase after a ball together. Having you down here at my level is fun for both of us.

I'm really enjoying my family in these months before my first birthday. I can tell the difference between my family and other people. I like my family best of all. I like playing, hugging, kissing and tickling. Playing during these five months is very important to me.

Sometime after my first birthday I'll go through a long period when we won't have so much fun together. That's why I hope we can play and laugh a lot now. I don't want to miss any fun!

Looking Ahead

The relative quiet of early infancy will come to an end during months 8—12. A more active and vigorous phase of life will begin for you and your baby after her first birthday.

Months 8—12 will be an active time for your child, like the toddler exploring nature at left.

Soon your baby will start moving around by scooting, crawling and eventually walking. She'll no longer be content confined to her crib or playpen for long periods. Her strong curiosity compels her to move around everywhere.

DEMANDING TIME

Exploration is exciting to your child. It can be demanding on you. Your baby learns to move around before she gains the judgment necessary to handle this new freedom. Her mobility will continue to develop faster than her judgment until she becomes a mature adult. You must decide how to encourage curiosity and exploration, while giving guidance and protection.

You'll want to put gates at the bottom and head of a stairway. Then choose a time of day when you open the gates for climbing.

Climb the stairs right along with your baby. Soon she will do it safely alone.

When your baby shows interest in cupboards, choose one where you will allow her to play. Put catches on other cupboards. Fill her cupboard with pots, pans, lids, muffin tins and other equipment. Make it a safe place to play.

MOBILITY

Your child may be frightened by her own mobility. This mobility is accompanied by *fears* that create conflicts within her. She may want to be on the move constantly, exploring things. But she also wants to be close to one parent, especially mother. She may want mother always in sight. Help your child deal with such conflicts by establishing closeness between your baby and *both* parents. Father should spend as much time as possible with his baby. He can take part in caring for her and playing with her. Having a close relationship can be personally rewarding for the father and your child.

BABY SITTER

Helping your baby develop a close relationship with a *baby sitter* can be important at this stage. Your baby's familiarity with other persons is important to you and your child. It will give you a chance to go out for a few hours. After much time spent with your baby, it will mean a great deal for you to be around adults.

A baby sitter will be important to your child, too. Your child will have one more person to interact with and to depend on. Your baby needs to learn that you are not the only person who can meet her needs.

ENCOURAGE CURIOSITY!

The importance of your baby's educational development beginning at about 8 months can't be overstated. This period lasts until the 3rd birthday. During these months, your child's basic attitudes toward herself and others begin to take shape. Her vigorous curiosity continues to grow. It should be encouraged. Any attempt to suppress her natural inquisitiveness can have a lifelong effect. *Assist your child in exploring and expressing her curiosity. It's one of the most important things you'll ever do for her education.*

DON'T FORCE EATING

Vigorous physical activity will sometimes interrupt your baby's eating and sleeping. You may often expect your baby to eat more than she wants or needs during months 8—12. *Don't attempt to coax or force her to eat when she's not really hungry!* This is one of the most common causes of feeding problems.

The ability to move about and explore is exciting for your youngster. Her immature skill can also create conflict. She may be attached to you, needing to be near you and keep you in sight. Yet she wants to discover what's around her. One way to cope with this problem is to establish a closeness between baby, mother and father. This gives her more opportunity to explore while fulfilling her need for closeness.

ANTICIPATE SCHEDULE CHANGES

When your baby's need for sleep decreases, be prepared to change her schedule. *Anticipate and adapt to her schedule changes by carefully observing her need for food and sleep.*

Don't expect more of your baby than she's capable of when she starts moving around the house. *Just because she's begun to walk and talk doesn't mean she's ready for toilet training!* She needs several more months before toilet training is begun.

BEWARE OF DANGERS!

Your child is just beginning to move around without constant supervision. This puts her in danger of injury from falls, poisons and choking. Her development can be so rapid that she finds dangers you never thought of. Suddenly she is able to open cabinets, crawl into closets or push open doors. If you haven't babyproofed your house as recommended on pages 45 and 60, you should do it now.

TEACH HER WHAT "NO" MEANS

During these months your child will begin to learn the meaning of "no." But she won't be mature enough for you to depend on these verbal restrictions to protect her from danger. You still need to preserve your prized possessions.

She must learn there are restrictions in life. Your use of the word "no" can help her understand these limits. *"No" should be used sparingly and consistently.* Whenever your baby is doing something dangerous to herself or others, simply say "no." *Don't use long explanations that will only confuse her at this age.* Never say "no" to any activity unless you are prepared to follow through. Always make sure your command is obeyed. *Repeat "no" a second time if necessary. If your child has not responded, calmly but firmly remove her or the prohibited object.*

It's important now and throughout child-rearing that both parents agree on rules. You need unity and consistency in teaching your child.

DON'T CONFUSE HER

It's important at this time to avoid confusing discipline. Your child will become confused if you say "no" to something and then don't follow up when she continues. She'll also have difficulty learning self-discipline unless you *teach* her consistent and firm discipline.

SPECIAL NEEDS

Here are some special needs that occur during months 8—12:
Personal Relationships—Your child is gaining independence, but

Teach the meaning of the word "no" so your child will understand society's rules. Be consistent when you say "no." If your child disobeys, act immediately so your instructions will be understood.

Increasing independence will characterize your child during these months. The desire for attention will diminish if you consistently meet the need for closeness. Your child must also understand what behavior is prohibited, like picking the neighbor's flowers!

Your child's need to explore may lead to unusual places. Ensure safety, but don't overprotect!

she still needs your attention. Clinging behavior, wanting you always in her sight and hanging on to your legs and clothing are not expressions of selfishness. She needs the security that comes from knowing you are near and available to help. Close attachment will usually be expressed toward mother. Other family members can help by playing with and sharing in the care of the child. Generally, *demand for attention will become less intense if your baby's need for close relationships is accepted and met.* The behavior will *intensify* if her demands go unful-

filled. Make your child feel secure. She won't demand so much of you.

Exploration—Your child has a real need to explore, touch and handle things. Curiosity signals the beginning of intelligent behavior. *Protect her, but don't overdo it.* Her desire to learn has its roots in curiosity. Her need to explore also includes playing and learning new games. The simple games you play with your baby are important to her education. This puts another demand on you. Remember, it's your baby's gain and your joy!

Limits—Your child's curiosity has virtually no limits. Her need to explore can lead her to danger if you don't impose restraints. She'll object, but restrictions are necessary for her safety. You should place as few physical restrictions as possible on your child's exploration. Her curiosity and learning will be encouraged by your understanding. *But she must also learn there are certain forbidden activities.*

Make a list of what is forbidden so that both parents say "no" to the same things. Even when a house is babyproofed, there are things that your child must not touch. She needs the security of knowing you won't allow her to touch dangerous objects. She also needs to know these precautions are for her own safety.

When your baby reaches her first birthday, her learning and development become rapid. You can almost see the changes day by day. Her personality and intellectual growth are important. This is a delightful time to share with your baby despite the demands on you. She can thrill you with accomplishments and charm you with love and adoration. She can also send you to bed exhausted each night. Her enjoyment of life makes it worthwhile.

About Your Child

Many things will happen during this period. In the 8th month, most children are still confined to the crib and playpen. They spend most of their time lying on their backs. By the 12th month, your child's mobility will extend throughout your house.

DIFFERENCES IN CHILDREN

Keep in mind differences that make children unique. Your baby may sleep little at night or in the daytime. Another child may sleep all night and take two naps during the day. Your baby may be active, curious and excited by new experiences and skills. She may resist bedtime and naptime. You have to learn how much rest and activity she needs. Don't be alarmed by her differences from other babies.

INDIVIDUALITY

Your baby has individual attitudes, behavior, interests and facial expressions. During months 8—12 she will become increasingly aware of herself as a distinct person. She may become possessive of you and family members. She will want your undivided attention. She won't want to share you with anyone. Her attachment will be strongest toward the one who provides primary care.

Accept and appreciate this possessive behavior even though your baby can't have your constant attention. Her clinging behavior should last only a few months. She will soon learn about herself and your dependability and availability.

Asserting independence will begin shortly after your child's first birthday. That's what all her present demands on you are leading up to. She's developing confidence and a sense of security. When she has those feelings, her clinging behavior will disappear.

A youngster won't always react happily when you are teaching limits to behavior. Don't let crying alter your judgment when you have to say "no."

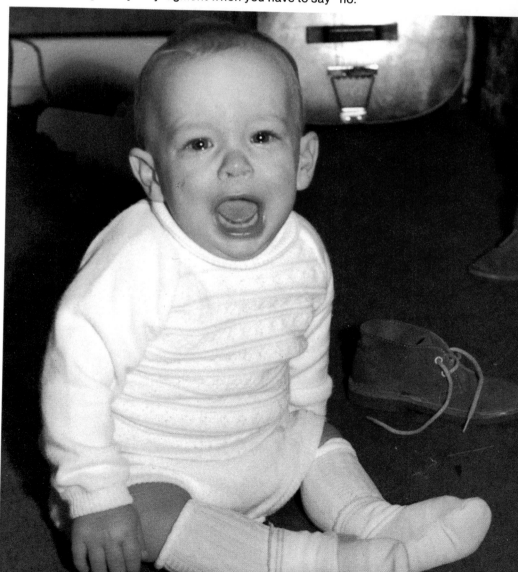

Tasting and examining food becomes a regular activity as soon as solid food is offered. Meals can become a real test of will between you and your baby. Your child needs a balanced diet, but realize that her tastes will change. This is a period of extreme messiness as you allow her to practice eating with a spoon. Learn what food she likes. Give her your support as she learns to feed herself. The day will come when her sloppy habits will be refined into proper eating skills.

Mouth and Eyes

Your baby will continue to put nearly everything she finds in her mouth. But now she's *tasting* to see if things are good to eat while exploring texture and shape.

MEALTIME BATTLEGROUND

Her eating behavior can become a major problem—a battleground for both of you. She will want to eat nearly everything she can get. Mealtime can become a conflict if you try to impose your adult ideas on her. *Follow your physician's advice and be sure your child receives a balanced diet. But recognize that there may be changes in what she wants to eat at mealtime.* Learn what tastes and textures she finds appealing.

Your child will go through growth spurts and periods of leveling off. These changes influence the amount of food she requires.

FEEDING HERSELF

Improved use of her hands will enable your child to learn to feed herself. *Provide food she can eat with her fingers. Let her begin using a spoon.* The results will be messy. Eventually she'll learn. Use metal spoons while your baby is learning. Don't use plastic spoons. They may crack when she bites them.

TEETHING IRRITATION

Teething may cause your baby to be irritable. She doesn't understand why her mouth is sore. *Make sure she has plenty of things to bite and chew on while her teeth are coming through.* Fingers are fine to chew on, but her new teeth are sharp. She'll need hard teething objects to help *file down* her sharp new teeth. Any of her *safe* toys will serve well as teething objects. You can give her zwieback bread or other firm foods. Suggestions are on page 48.

By 10 months most children have four upper and four lower teeth. *These teeth are used for biting, not for chewing.* Molars for chewing appear at about 1 year.

VISION CHANGES

Some changes are taking place in your child's vision. She spends a lot of time staring intensely at objects. She's trying to remember them completely.

Object Permanence—Your baby begins to realize during these months that objects exist even when she is not looking at them. This development is called *object permanence*. It's an important event in mental development.

Until this age, when a toy dropped out of sight it simply ceased to exist as far as your baby knew. Her improving memory now helps her remember these objects. When a toy drops out of sight, she'll look for it where she last saw it. Cover a toy with cloth. Your baby will lift up the cloth to find it. This can be the basis of an interesting and worthwhile game. She'll enjoy seeing toys appear and disappear, as if by magic. This game can be repeated many times until your child understands that these objects have permanence.

Object permanence also affects your baby's relationships with people. *She now remembers you*

  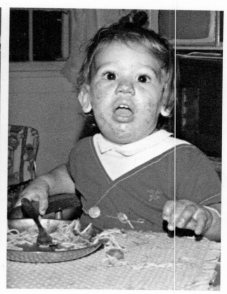

face and knows you are somewhere, even if she can't see you. Object permanence requires many months before it is fully developed. Your baby is not sure you'll reappear every time. Games like Peek-a-Boo and Hide-and-Seek will thrill and reinforce her. She will delight in discovering the magical appearance and disappearance of your face.

Manipulation

Your child will improve at reaching and grasping objects. She'll begin to coordinate her hands and eyes fairly accurately. She can see something, reach, grasp, retrieve and put the object in her mouth. Or she can hold it in her hands while examining it visually.

TOUCHING

The next major development is small but important. *Your baby will learn how to reach for an object and instead of grasping it, simply touch, stroke or pat it.* This is important because it allows her to learn about things that can't be grasped. *Now she can learn about texture and hardness.*

Touching, stroking or patting an object without actually grasping it becomes a great delight to your child. The art of feeling things is a primary learning tool.

Playing with blocks will lead to the skill of stacking. This may be possible by your child's first birthday. It's a complex muscular skill. Not all babies accomplish it at the same age. Stacking is usually done with the preferred hand, so this may show you which hand will be dominant. Don't try to change your child's hand preference! You can cause problems.

will be her exploring hand. The other will be used primarily as a holder. A few months ago, if you offered her a toy when she already held one, she would drop the first and reach for the second.

At about 10 months, she'll reach for a second toy while still holding the first in her other hand. If a third toy is offered while both hands are full, she'll drop one or both toys before reaching for the third. By her first birthday, your child can hold an object in one hand and place a second in the crook of her arm. Then she can reach for a third object with her free hand. She may continue to reach for additional objects as long as she can hold them.

RIGHT-HANDED OR LEFT-HANDED?

When your child starts walking, she may attempt to carry as many objects as possible. She will develop a preference for her reaching hand and holding hand. *Trying to make your child right-handed by always placing toys in her right hand does little good. This can frustrate her. Let her use both hands at this early age. She can't understand the meaning of right-handed or left-handed. She'll decide by experience which hand works best. Let her make the decision.*

STACKING BLOCKS

By her first birthday, your baby may have mastered stacking one block on top of another. This is a complex activity requiring visual and muscular control. Your baby may learn to stack blocks by imitating you. When she perfects the skill, she may spend a lot of time stacking blocks and watching them fall. Because it's a complicated action, her *preferred* or *dominant* hand is nearly always used for stacking. The other hand holds the additional blocks. By observing the stacking you can determine whether she is more likely to be left-handed, right-handed or *ambidextrous* (uses both hands equally well).

Your child will learn by feeling things. She will become increasingly interested in feeling through her fingertips. She'll stroke a tabletop, rub a blanket, feel a stuffed animal and stroke your hair. Before, when she put her hands in your hair, she pulled a handful. Now she'll be interested in *feeling* it.

Hand and finger skill will increase with practice. Soft cartilage in your baby's hands and wrists will be replaced with firm bones and strong muscles. The difficult task of eye-hand coordination will slowly be mastered. Crude sweeping motions of the hand will be replaced by a smoothly coordinated motion of arm and hand.

BOTH HANDS ARE BUSY

Your baby will begin to use each hand for different purposes. One

LEARNING BY IMITATION AND REPETITION

Until now most of your baby's physical discoveries were the result of accidental movements. They were interesting so she repeated them. When she held a rattle and shook it, a sound was made. She learned to shake the rattle to hear the sound. *Beginning in about the 8th month, your baby will watch your hands to see what you do. Then she'll intentionally try to repeat what she sees.*

She may become fascinated with the movement of your hands as you play with her toys. You may stack toy rings on a post, then take them off. Or you may push a toy car or pour water from a cup during her bath. Your baby will frequently try to repeat what you have done. *This ability to learn by imitation is an important educational accomplishment.*

Your child will learn a few things that can annoy you as her physical dexterity increases. She may learn to take off her shoes and socks. Before her first birthday, she may even learn to take off her clothes. Be patient with these little tricks. Remember that she's learning new skills. A few months later, she'll learn *when*

Much of what your child learns will be by imitation and repetition. Praise your youngster when she tries to imitate your mopping or dusting chores or when she wants to spade the garden. Your approval and praise will help establish an effective learning pattern.

and *where* it is proper to undress.

Your child's fascination with dropping and throwing objects will continue to be a source of frustration for you. Understand that her dropping and throwing are impor-

tant to learning. This will help reduce your frustration.

Tie toys to the edge of the crib or playpen with a piece of soft yarn. Your child can then learn to pull the toy back and throw it repeatedly. *Use yarn that will break easily if your baby becomes entangled in it. Never use anything that is strong enough to strangle or injure her.*

Social Development

At this stage your friendly, outgoing child is changing rapidly.

SHYNESS INCREASES

Your baby may become increasingly shy and withdrawn from other people. This may begin in about the 8th month and continue through 12 or 14 months. The baby who was always ready to go to anyone's outstretched arms may suddenly cling to you. She may hang on tightly to your neck whenever a strange face appears.

Stranger Anxiety—Shyness is common in children. But not

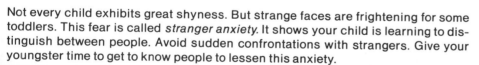

Not every child exhibits great shyness. But strange faces are frightening for some toddlers. This fear is called *stranger anxiety*. It shows your child is learning to distinguish between people. Avoid sudden confrontations with strangers. Give your youngster time to get to know people to lessen this anxiety.

During this five-month period your child may develop a close, demanding attachment to one person. This is usually mother if she is the primary food provider and caretaker. This attachment is part of the bonding process between parent and child.

every child experiences it to the same degree. Most children are attracted to any human face for the first six or seven months of life. As indicated on pages 9 and 10, fascination with the human face is common. Babies will stare at even a crude outline of a face. By about the 8th month, a period of shyness will begin for your baby. This is called *stranger anxiety.* This fear of strangers is an indication of your baby's advancing maturity. She can recognize familiar people as well as strangers. *Don't be upset by this sudden change in your baby's behavior. Recognize it as simply another normal step in her growth.*

Your child may cry if she is left alone with a stranger. This fear shows she is thinking and reasoning. But she doesn't understand her fear. She only knows that none of the *important people* are present and she's alone with a stranger.

If your child shows signs of stranger anxiety, tell her you will return. Be aware of this potential anxiety. Allow time for your child to get acquainted with strangers.

ATTACHMENT

Your baby will make intense social demands during this five-month period. The process of bonding that began at birth now centers around one special person. Usually it's the one who provides food and physical care. Most often this is mother. Your baby learns to know and demand this special person more than anyone else. She wants mother around all the time. She doesn't want to share her with anyone.

The relationship has changed from seeing the special person as a *caretaker* who simply provides food and care. Now there is a genuine feeling of affection. She'll want your presence constantly. She'll want to sit on your lap, cling to your legs and play with you. She'll want to pat your body with her hands and stick her fingers into your eyes, mouth and ears.

Possessiveness—Her possessiveness will be both delightful and irritating. Worshipful behavior is flattering and enjoyable. But possessive demands and incessant clinging can disturb you. *This is her first experience of affection. Accept and respond to it. Realize the intense emotions that are within her.* Eventually she'll feel secure that her love is accepted and you love her in return. She'll be less possessive and demanding when she truly feels this security. She'll soon let you leave her and feel confident you'll return.

Separation Anxiety—Fear that you'll disappear and not return is referred to as *separation anxiety.*

The frustration your baby feels is more intense if the concept of object permanence has not yet developed. See page 68.

The intense emotional attachment she feels for a special person often makes her terrified. She may think this person will simply disappear and not return. *If she's told the person will not disappear, your baby will become secure in feelings of love. She'll be able to bear separation for short periods of time.*

Little by little this security will grow. She'll have a firm basis for experiencing love and relationships with other people. This will occur if her needs are met during this crucial phase.

Your baby's social demands can disrupt her play and sleep. She may play contentedly for hours, then suddenly demand your attention. She may also cry at bedtime, not wanting you to leave her room. For a few months, your child's psychological need for your attention should be respected. *You may have to rearrange your schedule. Allow your child to be in the same room with you whenever she decides she needs you.*

When she's tired and should go to sleep, you may have to stay in her room. You can place your hand on her arm or leg until she falls asleep. She may awaken at night and be frightened that you have disappeared. Respond to her cries as quickly as possible and assure her of your presence. She'll probably be comforted enough to return to sleep.

If you respond to this anxiety by "letting her cry," this may make your child *more anxious* and *more afraid.* This anxiety may seem a burden, but it's brief. *What your child must have now is sympathy, understanding and your presence.*

Language

Months 8—12 are crucial to your child's language development. She may not speak a recognizable word before her first birthday. But she must *learn* language long before she can *speak* it.

Learning to speak is complicated and difficult. The most difficult task is understanding that sounds made with the mouth represent objects and ideas. Your child attempts to understand this by listening to others speak. During these months your baby will direct attention and concentration at your speech. *Help her by speaking to her as much as possible. Let your conversation be natural and normal. Use correct speech patterns and grammar.*

If you use baby talk, swear words or slang, you'll eventually be imitated. Your child needs good models of language.

SOUNDS REPRESENT OBJECTS

When your baby understands that the sounds you make represent objects and ideas, she'll attempt to understand. She wants to know which sounds represent particular things. Sounds that represent *ideas* are more difficult to comprehend at this age. Your child will pay more attention to sounds that represent names of familiar objects.

Comprehension Before Speech —Your baby will comprehend the meaning of many words before she speaks them. She'll try to produce the sounds once they are understood. The next step will be to actually speak sounds that represent an object. *Conscious speaking of words may occur around your child's first birthday.* There is a difference in the time when children begin to speak intelligible words. Some will understand a word and use it regularly. Others seem to learn meanings of many words long before they speak. Then they burst forth with the words all at once.

TALKING IS FUN!

Initially, your baby's speech is *not* for communication with you. Effective communication already exists between you and your child without spoken language. *Your baby will learn to talk for the sheer enjoyment of it.* The first words she'll use will probably be names of persons or things that are important to her.

Your baby will show interest in adult conversation at about the 8th month. She'll turn her head from person to person, staring intensely at each while he speaks. It appears that she understands what is being said. She'll occasionally make excited little sounds that are indications she wants to join the conversation. These sounds are not cries or screams. They are excited, intentional sounds that obviously mean "Pay attention to me! I want to be part of this conversation, too!" These sounds are the very first she'll make with the specific goal of communicating with others.

CONVERSATIONS

Sounds that your child makes will change dramatically about the 9th month. The babbling and cooing of earlier months will change into noises that vary in pitch and inflection. Her questions, statements and excited interjections sound much like speech. She'll sound like she's speaking a foreign language!

Jargoning—Your baby's speech in this stage is known as *jargoning.* This often occurs when she's alone or carrying on *conversations* with other people. She'll be listening and responding as if the interchange were a friendly chat. She gets obvious enjoyment from these jargon conversations. This indicates the importance she puts on learning to converse with others.

FIRST WORD

Your baby will probably use her first word sometime during these

This age level is vital to language development. Your child may be a year old before she speaks a word. Prior to speaking, she'll begin to *understand* words. When her first word does come, it may not be properly spoken but may have specific meaning.

five months. It will be different from the "mama," "dada," "baba" sounds that she has already used. Those were mere repetitions of sounds, uttered without understanding. This first word may not be one you will find in a dictionary. *Your child now understands that words represent objects. She creates new words to represent things.*

She may name a car "Mog." You'll know "Mog" means car because your child is consistent and excited about using the word. Gradually, by listening to you and other adults who speak properly, she'll identify the proper word for each object. *When she calls a car "Mog," share in her excitement! Don't correct her error. But don't call the car a "Mog" yourself.* Learning proper names for objects is difficult enough for your child. Don't make it more so by repeating her baby talk because it seems cute.

Love is the dominant emotion at this age. Respect your child's intense feelings. Be aware that *separation anxiety* and *stranger anxiety* can occur.

When she calls it "Mog," show your interest. Respond, "Yes, car!" *Subtle correction lets your child know that you understand her word. It also helps teach her the proper word.*

HELP YOUR BABY LEARN

This is the time to help your baby learn word meanings. She may not speak *any* words or may use only one or two before her first birthday. *The most effective way to do this is by talking and reading to her. Repeating the same word over and over is not very effective.* Repeating "Say shoe!" will not help her much with language. You are trying to teach a person, not a parrot! Your child will learn words most effectively by listening to your speech in natural conversation and play. One exciting game to a child is "Where is . . . ?"

You ask, *"Where is your nose?"*

"There it is!" you say with a smile as you and your child point to her nose.

"Where is the dog?"

"There he is!" you tell her as you both point to or touch your dog.

This game is effective for teaching language. Your baby will love it, and so will you!

Emotions

Love! It's the dominant emotion your baby will experience during months 8—12. There's a lot of joy in the emotional attachments between your baby and the family. The intensity of this love can create separation and stranger anxiety, which were discussed earlier. The emotional demands that love has placed on your baby should be respected.

NIGHTFRIGHT

Babies of this age often experience *nightfright.* Although no one can be sure, these are probably responses to dreams and nightmares. Your baby can't distinguish between real happenings and dreams. This explains her intense reactions to nightfright. During the night she may wake up howling with fear. *Sometimes these nightfrights continue for several months. When you hear this sudden cry of fear, go to your baby and reassure her as quickly as possible.* You might comfort her simply by touching her. She may return to sleep without being picked up. *Her cry of fear is a cry for help.* Respond to that cry quickly and completely. This will assure her of your concern and will help overcome her fears.

ANGER

Expressions of anger are not unusual in babies of this age. Her ability to move about is growing. Your baby can become angry when she's frustrated. She's still helpless in many ways. This feeling can add to the frustration. The difference between anger and fear is expressed clearly. You must distinguish between them and treat them differently.

Little Control—Your baby has strong emotions but little power to control them. When she's tired, a small frustration will sometimes cause a tantrum. *Your baby loses control of all emotions in a tantrum.* She may scream, bang her head and move her arms and legs violently. This loss of control is frightening to her and disturbing to you. *Respond by staying with her. Calm her by your presence and perhaps by placing your hand lightly but firmly on her stomach or chest.*

Why the Tantrums?—Tantrums occur for two reasons. First, they occur when situations become unbearable and your child falls apart emotionally. The possibility of controlling emotions no longer exists. You and your child have to wait out these periods. It will help her if you remain calm and loving. The other reason for a tantrum is more devious. Children want things immediately. They will learn that a tantrum may get them what they want. Then tantrums are a successful strategy. *Don't allow your child to learn this use of her temper.*

Don't Give In!—You should not attempt to distract her during this emotional outburst. Avoid giving in and allowing her to do what she originally wanted. She must have your support, but it should be consistent. *Teach your child that things can't be obtained by screaming and crying.* While waiting with your child for the anger to subside, try to recall the events that caused the tantrum. Avoid these in the future. There are limits to what a baby younger than 1 year old should be allowed to do. Your child is mobile and relatively free now. She doesn't understand the meaning of limits. Try to be patient while you teach her what she can and can't do. She's learning limits for the first time.

Motor Development

The months before the first birthday are filled with activity as your baby develops muscle control. Control of the major muscles progresses from her head down to her feet. Control of her neck muscles is first mastered. This prevents her head from wobbling like a rag doll when she's held. Next, the back and shoulder muscles develop so she can balance when seated alone.

Using the strength of her arm and shoulder muscles, your child will begin pulling herself to a standing position. This allows development of her leg muscles. At the same time, she learns to get on her hands and knees to exercise her leg and hip muscles. She does this by rocking back and forth. This muscle strength will eventually allow her to crawl.

CRUISING

While learning to crawl, your child will probably first learn to scoot or roll. She'll move around fairly rapidly. The next stage of development is called *cruising*. Your baby will stand by using a sturdy piece of furniture for support. Then she moves her hands across the furniture and slides her feet sideways. She cruises around anything that will support her weight. This requires both hands to be used for balance. Her legs are still wobbly. Much effort is required when all her body weight is placed on one leg.

Her muscles will develop strength. One hand will be able to hold a toy while the other hand maintains balance. Then she'll attempt to step without using her hands. But she will encounter a new difficulty. *She can stand alone. But she can't sit down without help!* Interest in standing and walking, plus development of muscle strength, will eventually allow her to take her first unaided steps.

STARTING TO WALK

Your child may be taking some steps alone by her first birthday. Or she may still need assistance. The months before her first birthday will be filled with intense physical activity. But remember, wide ranges of accomplishments are normal for children. *Your child's first steps are meaningful to you, not her. Don't be concerned if she isn't walking before her first birthday.* She must develop physically and practice a lot before she learns to walk. Relax and enjoy her progress.

Some normal children do not walk

Learning to walk may progress from crawling to cruising to unassisted steps. *Cruising,* as shown by the young girl above, is when the child supports herself on something with her hands while sliding her feet. One day she'll surprise you by taking off on her own!

until they are 15 or 16 months old. Others begin walking as early as 8 months. It's a routine event for your baby. When she's ready to walk, she'll walk.

Delays in Learning—Physical maturity and individuality cause differences in the age when children learn to walk. *It's possible your child may become fascinated with other aspects of her development. She may delay learning to walk while she explores other interests.*

Listening to various sounds and learning the meanings of words

can preoccupy your child. Otherwise she may be learning to walk. Or she may want to explore things with her eyes and attempt to understand the world visually. Her time may be spent looking at objects and pictures. She may want you to join her, pointing at objects for you to see.

Another activity that can delay walking is the use of her hands. She'll learn to pick up, throw, stack and physically handle everything in sight. *Movement* may capture her attention. If it does, she may spend every waking hour moving around. She'll explore everything she can reach.

Cautious or Bold?—Children have different *attitudes* toward walking. Your baby may be cautious. She'll learn to balance herself properly. She'll examine everything from her new upright perspective. Or she may rush headlong into walking, throwing herself into the act without concern for bumps and bruises.

Be prepared for whatever course your child takes. If she rushes into walking, she'll require more attention and supervision than if she approaches it cautiously.

CLIMBING

Your baby will also learn to climb during these months. At first she will only climb to a height of about 6 inches. By her first birthday she may be an experienced climber who can get on chairs, tables or kitchen counter tops. *She needs to practice climbing, but make sure she's safe from falls.*

These months before your baby's first birthday require more attention than any other time of her life. She needs the chance to explore safely to satisfy her curiosity and develop her muscles. You can't keep her confined to a playpen all the time. Whenever freedom to move around is allowed, your child can be destructive. She won't recognize what she has done.

Discovering Sexuality

Babies quickly discover that their hands and feet are something to explore, play with and get to know. In the same way they discover their genitals.

Babies rub their genitals or *masturbate* because it gives them a *pleasant* feeling. Just as it is fun to play with fingers and toes, it is pleasurable to play with genitals. *There is nothing wrong with this behavior. It is perfectly normal.*

ADULT TABOOS

Parents who are shocked by their child's fondling of genitals deny the baby's pleasure by adult taboos. It's unfortunate when a parent criticizes the baby and says, "You must not do that." The baby's first step at *discovering sexuality* has been spoiled. The baby is confused.

Every child masturbates. If not done excessively, it will have no bad effect. The bad effect comes from parents' disapproving attitudes. If parents forbid a child to explore her body, the child will get the message that there's something bad about her genitals. She'll probably masturbate anyway. She'll do it in secret and with a feeling of fear.

WHEN YOU'RE IN PUBLIC

Given your attitude about genital fondling, what will you do when the behavior goes public? You are at the grocery store or sitting together in the doctor's waiting room. Your child is bored and starts to play with her genitals. What could be more natural for a child in such a situation?

In our society such behavior is frowned on. You can quickly give your child a book to read or a toy from your bag. Explain calmly about behaviors that are *personal* and done only in *privacy*. The same goes for running outdoors nude. This is common behavior for small children.

Be calm and considerate as you teach your child what is socially acceptable and what is not. At first it's confusing to a small child. She wants to please you and will probably go along with your rules. Don't force her or punish her.

EXCESSIVE MASTURBATION

Most children masturbate only occasionally. Usually the other challenges of life are much more interesting. Children want to explore life beyond their own bodies. Some are not up to the challenges and turn to themselves for pleasure.

Young girls can learn from their mothers what it means to be female. This discovery includes the art of putting on lipstick.

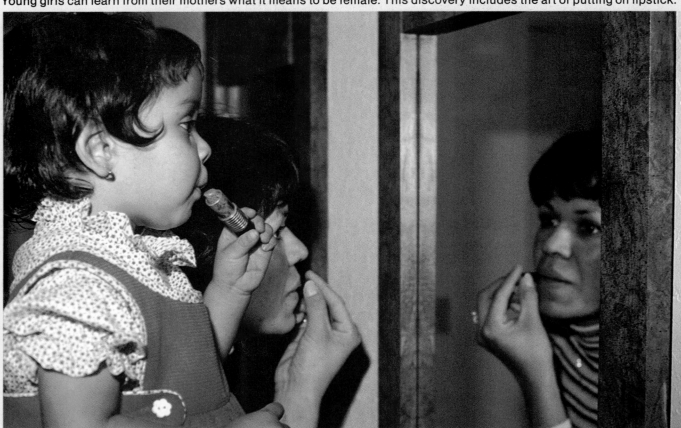

You may see your child spending more than a few minutes rubbing her genitals. Take a look at all the aspects of her life. Are there too many pressures on her? Are there enough interesting things for her to do? You can probably eliminate most excessive masturbation by correcting the overall situation.

SEX PLAY

When children around 30 months of age get together, a favorite game is playing doctor. This gives them a chance to explore their own bodies and their friends'. They may even fondle each other's genitals. They explore each other's bodies like they explore rolling and tumbling or playing Hide and Seek. It's natural behavior.

You may discover your child engaged in sexual play with friends. This will be a golden opportunity for an early lesson in sex education.

Spend a few moments with the children. You might open a casual conversation with something like, "I see that you've discovered each other's genitals and how boys and girls are different."

Answer all their questions honestly at a level they can understand. Don't confuse them with too much information. Follow the children's lead in questions and answers.

Depending on your tolerance for sex play, you will have to decide what you will allow and where and when. Discuss your rules in such a way that avoids punishment and guilt.

SEX IDENTITY

Toddlers will imitate their parents. Boys are likely to

When a young boy watches his father shave, the youngster is receiving an early lesson in manhood.

choose their fathers as models and girls to choose their mothers. The choosing of models occurs naturally unless a parent interferes. Boys discover they can stand up at the toilet just like their fathers. Girls discover that their mothers sit down. Boys try to copy the way father walks. Girls copy what mother does at the dressing table.

This will be an exciting time as your child tries to learn what it means to be a boy or girl. Observing both father and mother helps your child make distinctions. This may be a problem in single parent families. A grandparent, aunt, uncle or a family friend can be a good substitute. *Children do need models of both sexes.*

Balloons can be mouthed, manipulated, bounced and carried.

Pots and pans are for banging and stacking.

Pillows are good for throwing.

Selecting Toys

Many parents regard toys as innocent objects that merely entertain or help a child pass time. From the time your baby is born, your choice of toys can have great impact on her learning and development.

Regardless of your child's age, there are several things you should ask about toys: What can your child *do* with it? What *physical skill* or *mental activity* will it help her develop? Consider *safety:* Can she *swallow* it? Can edges *cut* or *puncture* her skin? Is it well made? Will it last?

Match toys to your child's skill level. If possible, *test* a toy on your child first to see if she enjoys it. Is she *challenged* by it? Does it *bore* or *frustrate* her?

Very *simple* objects often make excellent toys with high educational value. Many are available in your own home, or can be easily made. You'll face a challenge when selecting from thousands of commercial toys in stores.

Don't be misled by toys labeled "educational." Some commercial items are excellent for skill development. Others are not. You'll rarely have an expert nearby to consult. So be the final judge. Simply ask yourself the preceding questions about the toy. If you're not sure, find a toy you *know* will benefit your child.

The chart on the opposite page is a general guide to help you select toys according to your child's age level. Those suggested will stimulate her mind and help her progress in physical skills.

Stacking toys help develop muscles and manipulative abilities.

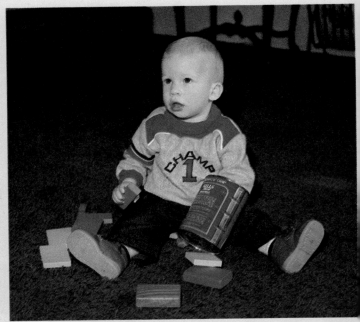

Let your child build with blocks and you can praise the work.

Scribbling and drawing are ways your child can be creative.

Toy trucks stimulate your youngster's imagination.

Feeding the doll is make-believe at its best.

Appropriate Toys for Your Child

You already have some of these toys in your home. Many can be made with simple materials. As your child grows older, you will think of many other ideas for toys. Observe your child playing with her toys. Make sure they are not too simple, boring or so complicated that she has failures.

	What your child can do	Toys	What toys mean to your child
Newborn	Looking	Mobile with changeable objects hung within 8-10 inches of child's eyes	Something to look at keeps baby interested in the environment.
	Listening	Clock tick-tocking Music box	Soothes the baby. Interests the baby.
3—6 months	Swiping	Mobile	Interests the baby; she learns that she can make it move.
	Grabbing Mouthing	Rattle, woolen ball, bean bag, stuffed animal, partially blown-up balloon, teething ring, wooden block	She now has some ability to explore her environment object by object.
6—12 months	Banging	Wooden blocks, lids of pots and pans	She can control the sound; learns about cause and effect.
	Dropping	All of the above toys plus plastic bottle or cup	Learns where things go when dropped or thrown.
	Casting or crude throwing	Balls, pillows	Practice in releasing objects.
	Pulling	Miniature pull cars	Learns about cause and effect.
Second Year	Climbing	Furniture, stairs	Practice for large muscles.
	Throwing	Balls	Eye-hand coordination.
	Emptying	Cups, jars	Eye-hand coordination. Early lesson in volume.
	Taking apart or fitting together	Stacking toys, nesting toys	Practice for muscles of manipulation. Opportunities for success in making things work.
	Pushing	Furniture, grocery cart, wheelbarrow	Practice for large muscles. Sense of purpose for child.
	Filling	Sandbox, boxes, cups, shovels	Further explorations with volume.
	Twisting	Screw lids, doorknobs	Exercises wrist muscles.
Third Year	Touching	Scrapbook of materials to feel	Learns about environment by touching.
	Drawing	Art materials	Pride in creativity.
	Building	Blocks, construction sets	Opportunities for manipulation. Pride in achievement.
	Make-believe	Costumes, doll house, dolls, small kitchen models, farm set	Opportunities for using imagination.
	Gymnastic playing	Climbing frame, slide, swing, balancing planks, tricycle	Practice for large muscles. Increasing height perception. Adventure.

Diary

Use these diary pages to record significant events and developments in your baby's growth or behavior. These records can be useful in understanding your baby as she matures. They'll also be fun to re-read months or even years later. Get to know your baby!

Months 8—9:

Diary

Months 10, 11 & 12:

About Your Child

Your child's self-awareness is increasing. Her feelings about the people, objects and routines in her life are also changing. Describe below her progress in feelings toward

Moving around, exploring:

Naps and bedtime:

Mother:

Father:

Other family members:

What is your child like at this age? Chart her characteristics below.

Characteristics	Often	Some-times	Rarely
Bold, headlong walker			
Careful, cautious walker			
Very active			
Content to play quietly			
Likes to visually inspect things			
Likes doing things with hands			
Likes two naps a day			
Wants to be with you constantly			

Mouth and Eyes
Months 8—12

Mealtime can develop into a messy problem at this age. Your baby is still learning, so try to understand her sloppy eating habits. How has her ability to eat with fingers and spoon progressed?

Describe your baby's progress in biting, tasting and swallowing food:

Are more teeth coming in? Number the teeth in order as they emerge:

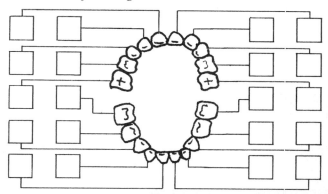

Does your child realize that lost objects or people still exist even though she can't see them? See object permanence, pages 68 and 69. What games does she enjoy that help her learn about object permanence?

Manipulation

Your baby's hand skills are improving dramatically. She's becoming more adept at using both hands. Describe her progress in

Touching and stroking:	Using each hand for different purposes:
Carrying objects in crook of her arm:	Stacking blocks:

At this age your child begins to learn by imitation and repetition. She will watch you do things with your hands. Then she'll imitate you. Describe below what imitative things she can do with her hands.

| Skill or activity | She is | |
	Adept	Not yet adept

Social Development

At about the 8th month your child may become shy and withdrawn with strangers. This is called *stranger anxiety*. Describe how she has reacted to new people during this period:

If your baby develops feelings of possessiveness, she may also show *separation anxiety*. This is a fear that you won't return when you leave her. Counter it with love and reassurance that you will return. Describe how your baby reacts when you leave:

Language
Months 8—12

Months 8—12 are an important period in your child's language development. She will comprehend many words long before she can speak them. List words you say to your baby that you know she understands:

Months 8—12 will probably be the period during which your child will say and understand her first words that represent objects. List those words here as she says them:

Subtle word corrections let your child know you understand her and also help teach her proper words. Describe how you have corrected your child's misuse of words.

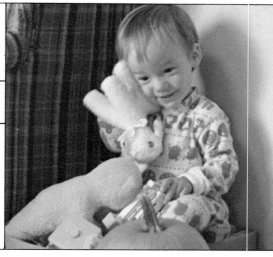

Method used	Worked	Did not work

Start a list of language games you and your child have played, such as reading and pointing. Rate each game according to its effectiveness in teaching.

Game	Effective	Fair	Ineffective

Emotions
Months 8—12

Love is your baby's dominant emotion at this age. She'll also exhibit fear and anger. Describe your child's cries, body movements and facial expressions when

Frightened:	Angry:

Frustrations may occasionally result in a tantrum by your child. Describe below her outbursts of emotion when she is tired or frustrated. Note what works best to calm her.

Motor Development

Your baby will become more mobile during months 8—12. By her first birthday she may progress from scooting and pushing to crawling, standing, cruising, climbing and even walking. Chart her progress below in those skills.

Month 8:	Month 9:	Month 10:

Month 11:	Month 12:

NOTE: YOUR CHILD IS INCREASINGLY MOBILE THESE DAYS! GO BACK AND REVIEW YOUR BABYPROOFING CHART ON PAGE 60.

Check Your Progress
Months 8—12

At the end of month 12, read through what you've recorded in the learning charts. Think about the progress you and your child have made. How are things going? Is her development proceeding smoothly? Use the chart below to check your progress and plan how you can guide your child in the coming months.

Area of development	Progressing very well	Could be doing better	Use the spaces below to plan what you can do to assist your child's growth and development in the areas indicated.
	Check one		
Personality			
Use of mouth and eyes			
Use of fingers and hands			
Relationships with others			
Language			
Emotions			
Ability to move around			

Months 13 — 16

Baby Talk

Now I'm a toddler! What a development! When I was an infant, I had to depend on you to bring things to me. But now I can get things myself and go where I want to. That means a lot to me.

I spent most of my life as an infant lying down. Now I can be up most of the time. Having this new independence is a great experience.

Some things may bother me during these months. If I'm cooped up or if I can't have something I want, I might have a temper tantrum. I still haven't learned to control my temper. I seem to fall apart emotionally when I'm frustrated.

Temper tantrums aren't much fun. The trouble is, I'm inexperienced. My refusals and shows of temper are just a way of finding out if they work. Whether they do or not depends on you. If you pay attention to my refusals and tantrums, I might keep using them. If you ignore them, I'll probably avoid that kind of behavior and try something else.

I hope you'll understand why I do things even when you say, "No, no." I feel so independent! I'll constantly test you to see what I can get away with. But it's not just you I'm testing. With all these new skills, I must test myself. Can I really walk by myself? Can I really climb onto your bed?

I hope you set limits on my behavior. This new independence is a little scary. It's not much fun to refuse your help at mealtime, then beg for it when I get tired.

Your caring and love are important to me. I'll do almost anything to get your attention. Please help me learn the right way to behave.

We'll have fun together if you can be patient and understanding during these confusing months. Let's play a lot of games. When I'm older I'll want to play with other children. Right now, I want to play with you because you play the way I like.

I hope you take pride in my walking. I want you to admire my exploring. When we go for a walk and I bring you a collection of pretty pebbles, praise my discovery. Don't say, "You're getting into everything!" I'm supposed to get into things! That's how I learn.

Your child is eager to learn. But for protection he requires limits to his behavior.

I need to improve two essential skills during these four months: walking and talking. These are important but difficult for me. I'm going to work on them one at a time.

We'll have a great four months if you can be understanding, loving and supportive. You mean more to me now than I can say.

Your toddler will show emotions more clearly at this age, like this youngster's love for her stuffed animal.

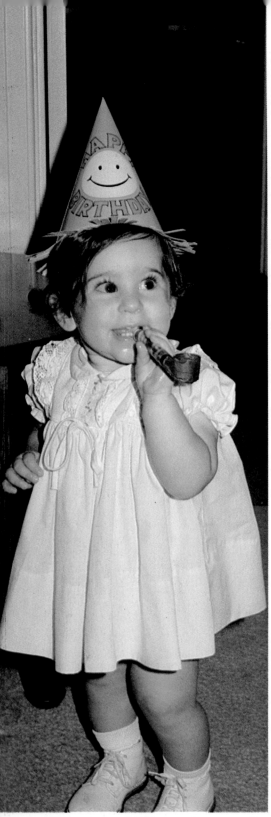

When your toddler enters months 13—16, you must be careful not to compare development with other children. At this age children may be very different in their skills. This is still a time of exploring and learning. It's a time for a parent to be supportive with a relaxed attitude.

Looking Ahead

Children of this age are difficult to describe because they differ so much. One child may not be walking yet, while another may be running. Some have a one- or two-word vocabulary. Others know several words. Some are aggressively independent. Others are dependent. There are a few children who are passive and quiet, but most are bundles of energy.

NO CHILD IS "AVERAGE"

The *norm* for children during months 13—16 describes what an *average* child will be like. *But remember, neither your child nor any other is average in all respects.* In the past 12 months, you've realized that your child's personality is unique. He's different from other children. His individuality will increase as he grows older.

The most apparent characteristic of this age is *high energy.* Your child may be all over the place, crawling, walking, running and climbing. He probably won't sit still for any length of time. His activities will be random. He'll dart from one activity to another for no apparent reason.

MUCH TO LEARN

He's *exploring* and *learning.* There is a great deal to learn. Your baby must be active in his environment in order to learn. He takes all the pots and pans out of the cupboard so he can bang them, fit them together and stack them. He'll pick flowers, collect odds and ends, climb ladders and try on your shoes. There's no predicting what he'll do.

You'll begin to see signs of learning by *perception* and *reasoning.* This is the basis of exploring and experimenting. Your child will experiment to see what happens. He'll also try things one way and then another to see if results differ.

Watch him in the highchair dropping food on the floor. If he looks carefully to see where each piece lands, then you'll know he's progressing mentally. He's learning from his experimentation, a behavior called *directed groping.* Watch as he fingerpaints on his tray, bib or clothes with his applesauce. His concentration and joy are amazing. Remember, he's *learning.* Forget the messiness of this experimenting. Relax and enjoy your child's progress.

SPECIAL NEEDS

Your toddler has the same needs at this age as in earlier months. Some needs have a new emphasis.

Understanding—Try to imagine that you are the first explorer on Mars. Your technical equipment is new to you. Your environment is alien. You are seeking knowledge about survival in a new environment. This exaggerated analogy explains your baby's situation. Consider what he faces. His motor skills of standing, walking, climbing and running are new. His environment is new. His understanding is immature. His only alternative is to learn by exploring and testing. That is your child's situation during these months. You'll be more prepared if you understand this need.

Your child has a message for you at this age: "Mom and Dad, I've got to find out what it's all about. I've got to do it my way. That's the only way I know."

Relax and *understand.* That's the key for this age level. Understand what's happening to your child. It will be easier for you both.

Protection—Babyproofing of your house must now be extended to your child's total surroundings. You may have to buy a harness to protect him from accidents when you're out walking or shopping. You may have to fence a yard area for safety.

You also need *to protect your child from frustrations.* Remove frustrating obstacles, such as the complicated puzzle from grandma. Don't introduce new or complex toys. Don't overwhelm your baby with such unnecessary demands as "Come to the table this instant."

Relax. Make life simple and slow down the pace.

Protect your child from fears. He understands more than you think. Before he can speak words, he'll understand them. If you talk about a frightening experience in his presence, you may cause him to learn a new fear.

Your child is living through a difficult time. He's getting around on his own, but he's still dependent on you.

Protect him from unnecessary obstacles. You'll have more fun together.

About Your Child

Getting to know your toddler is a challenge. He's growing as an individual. Realize and appreciate this adventure. It will continue as long as you communicate and as long as you learn more about each other.

Vision is important to your child's learning. Notice how he watches passing cars. Chances are that after one car has passed, his head will swivel in anticipation of the next. He's trying to learn and doesn't want to miss a trick. Watch how he tries to see what's behind him. He may bend over and look between his legs. Also notice how he intentionally drops things and looks to see where they land. During these months he may be obsessed with picking up tiny objects. This is his way of practicing eye-hand coordination.

The ability to see small differences makes it possible for your child to recognize things and people. He must experiment in order to adjust socially. Another baby is just an object until your child pokes or bangs him and receives a scream or hit in return.

Learning to talk also adds to his social action. By the end of this period your child may use a half dozen words. He may also use gestures to communicate desires.

Your baby will imitate as a way to learn social behavior. One of his best social skills is smiling. Encourage smiling rather than crying.

Understand your child's intense need to learn. Protect him from physical and emotional dangers. You'll enjoy your child's early development much more if you are patient.

LEARNING RIGHT AND WRONG

Your child is developing a *sense of right and wrong.* Teach him what is permitted, what isn't and how to *wait* for things. It's too early to expect sympathy for your hectic life and respect for your needs. Your child is too wrapped up in his own needs. But you can begin preparing your child for *later* sympathy and respect of others.

Reward Good Behavior—Your child will learn to repeat an activity that brings pleasure and avoid one that brings displeasure.

Reward desired behavior. Don't reward undesired behavior. Teach your child to distinguish right from wrong and use energy constructively. See the chart on page 106.

There is a direct relationship between the words *discipline* and *disciple,* meaning a *follower.* Your aim is to guide your child, so he must

Feeding problems can arise if you fail to realize that eating, and especially *tasting,* are learning processes. Your child will develop certain likes and dislikes. He may insist on feeding himself. Give him a chance to satisfy his curiosity as well as his developing appetite and taste.

be willing to follow. You assure this by praising the good things he does. Be sure not to reward bad behavior. Ignore it if possible, or at most say you don't like bad behavior. Your child will get the point.

Mouth and Eyes

Your child will master a number of new, important abilities with his mouth and eyes. This will occur during the months following his first birthday. At first he may open his mouth when he sees his cup. But he will learn to close it until the cup actually reaches his mouth. This behavior comes naturally. You can't force him. Learning to drink from a cup takes time, possibly several months. Let your child try. He may insist on it in his struggle for independence!

Tasting is another area of *sensory learning.* When your child tastes a new food, he may *like* or *dislike* it. The process is a way of learning. Many feeding problems begin during months 13—16.

It is natural for a child to cut down the amount of food he eats. Once he can walk, climb and explore on his own, there are more fun things to do than eat.

Your child may resist being fed by you. He'll want to do it himself. This can be upsetting, so relax and forget about teaching table manners for the time being. Don't worry if your child doesn't eat for a couple of meals or so. When he becomes hungry, he'll let you know. *Your goal is a happy baby, not a fat baby.*

ABILITY TO SCAN

Your child will develop a new visual ability. *When he holds something with both hands, his eyes can look for another object.* This was not possible before. It frees him to keep track of more things that happen around him.

LOOKING BEHIND

Looking behind himself is another skill your child will learn. Looking between his legs in a

The ability to look in many directions is a skill your child will eventually acquire. Bending over and looking between the legs will give way to turning the head or body around to see.

Drinking from a cup is harder than it looks, especially when you are 14 months old. Doing it gracefully comes only when your child has the chance to practice. That means you have to be ready for spills and sticky messes.

bent-over position will give way to turning his head or whole body. There is more to seeing than just using the eyes. You'll want to encourage his *intentional* looking. "Look" and "see" may become part of his vocabulary. You may often get pulled or pushed to see something.

SEE AND LEARN GAMES

Simple games will encourage your child to use his sight for learning. Ask him to point to "something big and white that keeps our food cold." Or he can find "something that helps in washing the dishes." Another game is Hide and Seek. You and he alternate hiding an object and seeking it. Follow the Leader is

another game that requires intentional looking.

Manipulation

Your child is learning to do many things with his hands that were impossible before. When he reaches for an object, his hands will land right on it.

CUPS AND SPOONS

Gracefulness in drinking from a cup will come gradually. At first, your child may hold the cup with both hands. Then he may use his thumbs and forefingers. Finally, he'll use one hand.

Using a spoon is tricky. It is easy for your child to hang onto the spoon, but difficult to lift it to his mouth without spilling food.

THROWING

Your child won't have much trouble holding a bottle if he's bottle feeding. Be prepared for him to throw it when he's finished. All objects will be candidates for throwing.

His ability to throw involves learning to *release* at the right time. Next, his *aiming* must be brought under control. He may begin by throwing things up in the air. Then gradually, with a clumsy, casting motion, he'll learn to throw *horizontally.* It's still early to expect accurate throwing. That will come in time.

BALL GAMES

Games with balls are favorites at this age. They'll be simple, but

Few toys are more fun than balls for learning simple skills. Balls can help your child learn to throw. They will also improve hand and arm coordination.

Scribbling is an activity your child will enjoy. Praise him for good behavior and good work. Have plenty of paper available. Be sure he knows where scribbling is permitted.

they give your child throwing practice. Begin by rolling the ball back and forth on the floor. Later, try throwing the ball into a basket or other large container. Your child probably isn't ready yet for pitching and catching. Learning to catch is difficult. Match games to your child's level of development.

SCRIBBLING

Your child will begin to scribble on paper now that he grasps well. His scribbles aren't pictures, but they help him realize he can make marks. Scribbles come in all shapes and sizes. The most common are slash marks across the paper. Some toddlers fill up an entire sheet with these marks. Keep lots of paper available. Fat crayons are better than skinny pencils while his muscles are still developing.

Show him where scribbling is permitted and where it isn't. You'll probably get a few scribbles on the wall. Let him know you don't like it. You can tape up large sheets of poster paper on the refrigerator or wall and let him practice. You can also play a game where one of you makes a mark, then the other imitates. Don't get ahead of him with *your* art work. Stay on his level.

He'll begin to distinguish between circles and squares. Toward the end of this period, he may be able to put a round block into a form board. These are usually available at toy stores. Form boards can also be made at home by cutting shapes out of plywood. Sand the pieces so your child can get them in and out easily.

TALLER BLOCK TOWERS

Ability to stack will also improve. First, one block will be put on top of another. A three-block tower may be possible at 16 months. Your baby will improve at carrying several small objects and transferring them from hand to hand.

All of your child's hand and finger abilities require practice. It looks like play to you. To your child it is work and learning. Give him plenty of opportunities to develop the small muscles necessary for using his hands. He *must* handle small objects in order to learn. He must get his hands on eating utensils and toys as well as faucet handles, doorknobs and switches. It's exciting for him as he develops these abilities and gains control. Take pride in him at each new success!

It's probably still too early to tell if your child is left- or right-handed. He may be using both hands or changing back and forth. *Hand preference will become more apparent closer to the end of the second year.*

Social Development

Your baby will emerge as a *social creature* during these exciting months. He'll start by being able to *tell people apart.* Then he'll be capable of a high degree of *interaction with people.* Previously, most of his concentration was on objects. Now the focus shifts to people.

SOCIAL GROWTH IS SLOW

Your help and understanding will be needed as your child slowly develops social skills. There's much to be learned! Be prepared for continued periods of shyness. *Your child may become sensitive or even suspicious.* His ability to recognize people will increase.

SCARY, HAIRY GIANTS

How would you feel if you had never noticed a bald head, a beard or a 200-pound giant before? Your baby will need time to look at people and adjust. You can help by taking him places where he can watch people at a distance. A park or playground is good. So are stores that aren't crowded and confusing.

Don't push your child into meeting strangers. Let it come gradually at his own pace. Be patient. Periods of shyness are usually followed by

Your child is able to stack more blocks at this age. It takes practice to get fingers and hands working skillfully.

This probably will be a period of great social activity for your toddler. He will become increasingly good at telling people apart. It could also be a time for continued shyness when your child may become sensitive or suspicious.

Putting toddlers together has some social benefits for each child, but they really can't interact much at this age. They play *alongside* each other rather than together. This is called *parallel play.* You are your baby's best playmate for now. Babies of this age can innocently harm each other with well-meaning pats. Be on guard when your child is placed with another.

periods of social interaction. This is often true if your child has not been forced beyond his own pace.

GETTING TODDLERS TOGETHER

Your toddler can benefit from being with other children. It's too early to expect much interaction. *Parallel play* is the term used for two toddlers playing *alongside* each other. They are aware of each other, but it will be many months before playing *together* begins.

You are your baby's best playmate at this stage because you're more familiar to him. You know how he likes to play and what he wants from game playing. Consider the game where your toddler hands an object to you. Another child wouldn't give the object back. But you will, and that's what your baby expects.

BABY BATTLES

Unless your child has had experience with babies, he views another baby *only as an object.* Parents are often horrified when their child pokes, pushes or hits a baby. *Your child will learn that other*

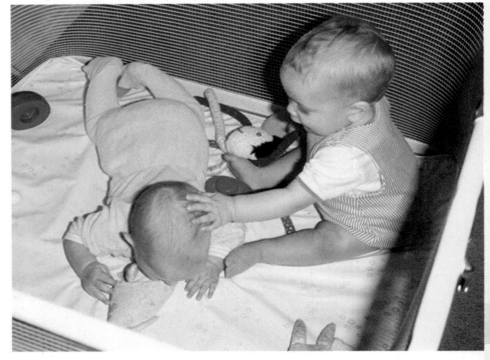

babies are people who scream and hit back or cry and crawl away. This is a normal process of learning. You'll have to guard against physical injury. Show gentleness with other babies so your child can imitate.

FIRST INTERACTIONS

Poking another baby is a social act on your child's part. Here are social activities that may represent your child's first interactions with people: (1) *holding your hand or*

You and your child can have great fun and build a deep relationship by laughing together. Now is the age to teach your child to laugh off minor bumps and bruises.

finger while walking, (2) putting a hand on a friendly stranger's knee, (3) imitating your behavior in doing household tasks.

In the first part of the second year, your child will want your personal attention in large doses. He'll go to extremes to get it. He'll flirt, dance, make faces and do other tricks for an appreciative audience. He may even develop stunts and perform repeatedly. If he does, he'll make important progress in dealing with people. Your support and encouragement will help him. He will gain the confidence to expand the number of people he can deal with.

LAUGHING IS IMPORTANT

Games like Hide and Seek, Riding Piggy Back and Follow the Leader contribute to social skills. You and your child can have fun together and lots of laughs. Laugh-

ing is important. It's a sign that your child is developing a sense of humor. This is helpful for social growth and acceptance.

There will be times when you don't understand why your child is laughing. Usually his laughing concerns something slightly unfamiliar or unexpected. Try looking in a mirror and making a funny face. Your child will probably giggle. You can make a game by taking turns. Each of you can make funny faces. Put on crazy hats. Imitate other people. Whatever you do, *encourage your child's laughter.*

LAUGH OFF MINOR BUMPS

Encourage your child to *laugh off minor bumps and bruises.* Often a parent will smother a slightly injured child with caresses, kisses and "poor baby." It's more appropriate to say "Let's blow away the hurt and play a game." Then you can laugh together and continue having fun. If your baby is really hurt, he'll need your immediate attention and love.

Language

There is more to mastery of language than merely learning to say words. At the beginning of this age period, your child may use *one*

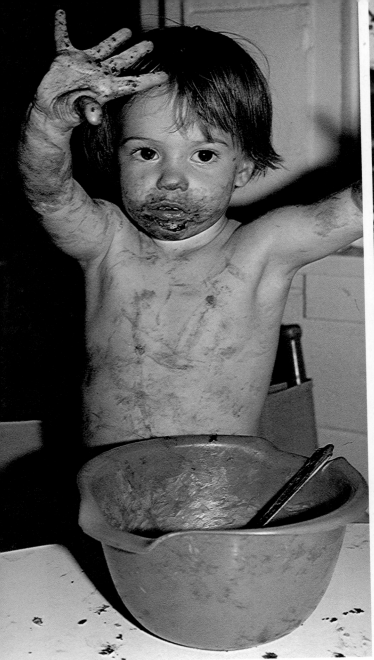

Often your child will need no words to convey important messages or meanings. Gestures and body language may say, "Now I've had my fill of cake batter and I want to wash." Or, "Over there's a bird that looks interesting to me." Gestures like these are steps toward learning to talk.

or *two* words. At the end his vocabulary may include *six to eight* words. That's not a big increase. His vocabulary may be up to *100 or 200* words by the beginning of his third year. But don't be discouraged. Much is happening to your child during these four months.

WALK OR TALK?

When children begin walking it's as though talking is put on hold. Walking and talking are so important that one is all your child can manage at a time. Vocabulary will increase greatly after walking

is mastered. *Your child may pu talking before walking or be able t handle both at once. Most childre delay speaking more than a word o two until the last half of the secon year.*

NONVERBAL COMMUNICATION

There are ways of communica ing that don't require word You'll probably hear the sam conversation-like jargon fror your child as you have for man months.

Imitations—Children are goo imitators. There are many noise

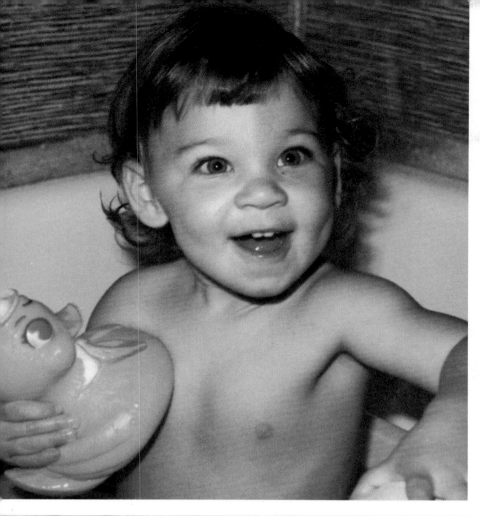

they can imitate to communicate with other people. They'll imitate coughs, nose blowing, sirens, airplanes, animals, music and much more.

Body Language—You may be pulled to the cupboard where crackers are stored. Your child may *point* and *push* as if to say, "I want a cracker." Or you may be presented with a collection of shells spread out on your lap. Your child's gestures seem to say, "Look what wonders I found!"

WORDS

Gradually your baby will learn that words are better for communicating. Single words come first. He may say, "Give!" and point at something. He means "Give me that toy." You should set *good examples* as your child's first words appear. Your speech will have great influence on his.

No More Baby Talk—Remember, children imitate. *If you've been using baby talk, stop.* Say words correctly, clearly and slowly. Use gestures to increase his understanding. "Put the cup on the table" is clear to you. But your child will understand better if you point first to the cup, then to the table as you say the words. Word-and-gesture training will interest and delight him. Your request will probably be carried out.

Words are better than gestures for communicating, as your child will soon learn. Playtime in the bathtub or an outing in the mountains may produce new words. Don't forget that your child is an expert imitator. If you've been using baby talk, stop the practice now. It will inhibit your child's language progress.

Your child can learn fears in two ways: from experience, or from other people. If your child is frightened by a dog, it's an experience that may lead to a general fear of animals. Give your child physical reassurance. Try to replace a fear with a good feeling, just as this family is doing.

You can be a great help to your child during these months. Language development is essential for his future. Your attention to his language will ensure that the foundations you build will support good language habits in the months ahead.

Emotions

Your child will show fear, disgust, anger, distress, excitement and delight before he is 1 year old. During months 13—16 his emotions will be even more clear. As your baby learns to recognize the difference between adults and children, he may be frightened by some people. He may feel friendly toward others. Previously, all people were liked or disliked as a class.

FEARS

Fears learned by your child are of two types:

Fears from Experience—If your child is bitten by a dog, he learns to fear dogs.

Fears from Other People—If you show certain fears, your child will learn them by imitation.

There are two ways to handle his fears. *First, give him physical reassurance.* Don't shame him. Comfort him physically. Verbal explanations won't do much good. *Second, try to replace a fear with a good feeling.* If your child is afraid of the dark, install a night light or tell simple stories about animals loving the dark. Go for night walks. Admire the moon and stars together.

FEAR OF LOSING PARENTS

Another common fear is that of losing parents. Your child has learned to love mother and father as the ones who provide his needs. Fear of losing you is serious. But you deserve time off despite this fear. There are ways to take it without increasing your child's fear of losing you.

Hire a dependable, loving baby sitter. Let your child become accustomed to the sitter while you

UNDERSTANDING AND RESPONSE

Your child understands the meanings of many words. He can look in the appropriate place when you say, "Where is the ball?" He'll respond to the request, "Give me the ball." He'll respond to his own name and gradually learn to respond when he hears the names of others. Much is happening in his language development even though his vocabulary is small.

COMMUNICATION CRISIS

A communication crisis can occur for your child, usually during the 16th month. But it can come earlier or later. It's related to his growing independence as a person and his *lack* of independence in language. Without the freedom of being understood through spoken language, he's still *dependent.*

Consider his plight. He can run around and get into all sorts of things. He can put toys together and take them apart. He can build small towers with his blocks and draw lines on paper, maybe even some crude circles. He has a number of new skills. Despite these talents he knows few words and others don't understand him when he talks. It's frustrating. No wonder he resorts to pushing, pulling, pointing, crying or having a tantrum!

This crisis may build gradually. Then it slowly subsides as his language abilities increase. Understand the crisis and you'll be able to deal with it effectively.

Take Time to Listen—Don't shrug off your child because you have difficulty understanding his first words. *Take time to listen carefully to words and gestures.* When he says "wawa," respond with "Do you want water?" *Never criticize your child. Correct him lovingly and tactfully. Your aim is to help him learn, not make him feel incapable.* If he screams "ba, ba, ba" and his gestures tell you he wants a ball, say "Do you want your ball?" Wait, if possible, for him to say "ball" before you give it to him. Be careful to keep his frustration level low.

are still around. Explain to your child that you'll be gone for a while, but you'll return. *Make first separations short. Don't leave while he is asleep.* His anxiety on awakening and finding you gone can be unpleasant. How is he to trust you thereafter? It's a good idea to plan separations in advance. Teach your child and the sitter some games they can play while you're away.

ANGER AND FRUSTRATION

Anger due to frustration is common. There are still many things your child is not able to do. He may want to move furniture, but the piano is frustratingly heavy. Puzzles with more than a couple of pieces are too complicated. Fortunately, his attention is easily diverted. When he becomes frustrated, redirect his attention to another activity. Do this before howls or a temper tantrum occurs. Some tantrums are unavoidable. It often helps to pick up your child and hold him close. Physical contact has a soothing effect.

RESTRAINTS

Restraints are also frustrating. Your toddler may hate to be dressed because it interferes with more fun things to do. A small toy for him to play with may help while you dress him. Some frustrations, like stopping play to be dressed, are inevitable. Your child is old enough to cope with them. He can recognize your emotions and will usually want to please you. *Reward him whenever he accepts the restraints and frustrations you must temporarily place on him.*

JEALOUSY

If a new baby is on the way, prepare your toddler so he won't be jealous when the baby appears. You can expect jealousy. Your child may wonder why he doesn't get your full attention and love anymore.

Begin dealing with this during pregnancy. Let your toddler feel the baby move. Let him help you with the baby's furniture, clothes,

bedclothes and diapers. Praise him for all his work. This will make him feel important. It may help eliminate feelings of jealousy when the baby arrives.

JOYFUL EMOTIONS

Your child will have positive emotions during months 13—16. You should solve problems with love and understanding as they occur. *Concentrate on your child's numerous expressions of excitement and delight.* He'll be excited when he first learns to walk, run and climb. He'll be excited when he learns that the duck floats in the bathtub. He'll love the wonderful sounds that occur when pans are pounded together. Such experiences are a joy for your child.

Accomplishments also bring delight to your toddler. Pulling or pushing a toy along the floor is a delight. Displaying a piece of paper with scribbling on it is a delight. Finger painting, sand play and water play are delights.

Concentrate on these happy moments. *Have fun with your child. Show him you are excited and delighted, too.*

Motor Development

You may think your child is a perpetual motion machine. He is, indeed, a young explorer. Crawling, standing, walking and climbing are being perfected. He can get around better than he used to. Add to that his natural curiosity and he becomes a real adventurer. *Your child must explore. Objects must be looked at, listened to, felt, tasted and smelled.* He must learn through his senses and through experiences.

Children start walking at different ages. This depends on growth and opportunity. Your child will probably walk by the end of his 16th month, if not sooner. But he may still resort to crawling at times. He'll learn to climb whether he can walk or not. A babyproofed house is essential during this period. If you haven't

removed the dangers and valuables, then you'll have to supervise your baby constantly. This will be in addition to numerous "no-nos." It's difficult for you and not very encouraging for him.

Your toddler will be persistent about walking, pushing, pulling and climbing. Persistence is important to his learning ability. Encourage him to practice.

TOYS THAT TEACH

Toys on wheels that your baby can sit on and propel with his feet are favorites as he nears the 16th month. Before that time, many objects around the house will make good toys. See pages 78 and 79. *Nested plastic mixing bowls, clothespins, boxes, spoons and cups are excellent.* He'll like to put one thing into another and take it out again. He'll put things together and take them apart. He'll like to pull and push. Let him push his stroller or help you push the grocery cart.

Toys with rings that fit on a spindle are excellent. At first, putting the rings on the spindle in any order is an achievement. By the 16th month he'll probably put the rings on in order of size. He'll like puzzles with only a few pieces.

SELECT TOYS CAREFULLY

Gradually, he'll begin to enjoy different form boards and geometric shapes. Always watch your child before introducing a new toy. You can judge if he'll enjoy it and be successful with it. Failures are frustrating, and they cause anger. *Successes teach your child good feelings about himself. Ensuring his successes should be one of your major goals as a parent.*

Discipline

Establishing a pattern of *discipline* with your child can be accomplished fairly easily. You must make a distinction between discipline, or training that produces acceptable behavior, and *punishment*, which means a harsh penalty for misbehavior.

Your preschooler won't become mature and trustworthy if he is punished harshly or slapped. Yelling, nagging or shaming won't work either. He'll gain maturity by being *loved, respected, understood and praised for his successes.* If his needs have been met, he will want to please his parents.

The purpose of discipline is to teach your child how to behave acceptably even when you are not around. This requires some *self-discipline.* Your baby will not have any self-discipline at first. He needs your help.

By age 30 months some children will have a certain amount of self-discipline. Some can be trusted not to cross the street alone or not to pick the neighbor's flowers.

SPOILING YOUR CHILD

You can't spoil your child simply by meeting his genuine needs. You *can* spoil him by shaming him, physically assaulting him or making him feel angry and unloved. He may fight back and try to take the power away from you by having a tantrum. He may throw things or kick you.

NOBODY'S PERFECT

No parent is perfect. There will be times when you'll lose your temper. There will be times when you'll scream.

If you want a well-behaved child, you must teach discipline. A child who is loved, respected, understood and praised for his successes will develop self-discipline. Your child will want to please you with good behavior if you meet his genuine needs.

Losing control of your emotions will not help your child. But an occasional display of temper won't hurt him much either, as long as it doesn't occur too often. Your child is resilient. As long as he knows you love him, he'll have the security he desperately needs.

This chart is a guide to help you understand and react to typical behavior by your child. It also tells you how *not* to react.

Common Discipline Situations

Situation	Understanding your child	What you SHOULD do	What you SHOULD NOT do
Temper tantrums	Your child is overpowered by intense emotions he can't control or understand.	1. Lift him up so that he does not injure himself or others. 2. *Wait calmly* until the rage subsides. 3. Divert his attention to an activity where he can have a success that you can *praise*.	1. Do not yell at him to stop. 2. Do not try to reason with him. 3. Do not leave him alone. He needs you with him. 4. Do not get excited. He needs you to be calm.
Throwing his bottle on the floor	He may be practicing throwing skills. He may be experimenting to see where it lands.	1. Pick up his bottle for him. 2. Tie a string to his bottle so he can pull it back himself. 3. If he threw his bottle to test you, pick it up and say, "I love you, but I don't like it when you throw your bottle on the floor."	1. Do not scold him. 2. If he threw his bottle on purpose to test you, do not spank him.
Breaking your favorite dish and blaming his brother	If he doesn't understand the concept of possession, he doesn't know that he has committed a misdeed. See pages 121 and 122. If he understands that you are sad about your dish, the burden of taking the blame is intolerable. That's why he blames someone else.	1. You have every right to say, "Oh, my favorite dish!" 2. Ask him to join you as you try to glue the pieces together. 3. Accept responsibility for leaving the dish in a vulnerable place.	1. Do not break one of his favorite toys. It starts a vicious cycle. 2. Do not force him to admit his guilt. He'll feel unloved and miserable. 3. Do not brand him as a liar. He won't understand anyway. He can't distinguish between make-believe and reality.
Crying the first time he goes to the beach or lake	He is not misbehaving. The ocean or lake is so big that he is frightened.	1. Show him the fun he can have in the sand. 2. Let him watch others having fun in the water. 3. When he is ready for a first test of the water, hold his hand and stay right with him.	1. Do not shame him for being a crybaby. 2. Do not force him to go into the water.

Rules about Discipline

Keep rules to a minimum. A rule about staying out of the street is essential. However, a rule about being neat at mealtime may not be necessary.

Be firm. Once you make an essential rule, stick by it. If the neighbor's rose garden is off limits, it's *always* off limits.

Be consistent. Don't ignore minor bumps and bruises one day, then go along with crying over a slight hurt the next day.

Praise desired behavior. When your child waits for a cracker while you finish on the phone, say "Thank you for waiting" and add a hug and smile.

Don't encourage undesired behavior. When your child says no to your request, respond with "I do not like it when you say no."

Be loving. As long as your child feels the security of your love, his reaction to discipline will probably be positive. *When he is denied love, his fragile world breaks apart and his reaction to discipline becomes random.*

Adapt discipline to your child. As you get to know him well, you'll find the best way to praise his good behavior. He may like hugs and kisses. But not all toddlers do. A reward of a small box of raisins may work wonders. Watch him to see what works best.

Diary
Months 13—16

Use these diary pages to record significant events and developments in your baby's growth or behavior. These records can be useful in understanding your baby as he matures. They'll also be fun to re-read months or even years later. Get to know your baby!

Month 13:

Month 14:

Month 15:

Month 16:

About Your Child

Setting a few, simple rules will work wonders with your child's behavior. What rules have you established in your home?

It is up to you to reward your child's desired behavior. Do *not* encourage *undesired* behavior. What are the best ways you have found to reward your child's good behavior?

Mouth and Eyes

The ability to taste will probably lead to distinct preferences for certain foods. List some below.

Food your baby likes:	Food he doesn't like:

Look and *see* may quickly become part of your child's vocabulary as his interest in looking and exploring increases. He will probably pull or push you to see something of interest. Record those objects here.

There are many simple games you can play to encourage your child's visual learning. Describe his behavior when you play pointing games, Hide and Seek, Follow the Leader or other games:

Manipulation

Months 13—16

How have your child's manipulation abilities changed since his first birthday? Describe the progress he has made during months 13—16.

Skill	Progress
Holding and drinking from cup	
Eating with spoon	
Holding and drinking from bottle	
Throwing objects	
Building with blocks	
Scribbling with crayons	
Using doorknobs	
Working switches	
Turning faucets	

Social Development

Your child's social relationships may become more open during these months. But he shouldn't be pushed. Describe progress in his association with

Mother:

Strangers:

Father:

Other toddlers:

Brothers and sisters:

Has your child learned to laugh and show a sense of humor? List objects, persons or situations that your child finds funny:

Language
Months 13—16

Is your child's list of words increasing? Chart his progress below.

Language development	At 13 months	At 16 months	
Words *spoken* and understood			
Words *understood*, but not spoken			
Difficult words that *frustrate*			

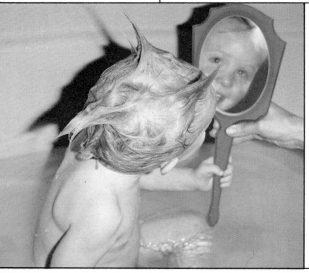

Your child will learn means other than words to communicate. Describe the body language and gestures he uses to convey his wants or needs:

Learning to imitate noises is part of your child's language development. List below the noises he imitates, or attempts:

Emotions
Months 13—16

This age period will be one of wide emotional range for your child. List the situations, people, objects or games that arouse excitement or delight in your child:

There are generally two ways your child can learn fears: from *experience* and from *other people*. List your child's fears and describe what you've done to help counter them.

Type of fears	What have you done to help your child cope with the fear?
Fears learned from experience:	
Fears learned from others:	

Does your child become angry and frustrated? List situations that cause these emotions in him:

Motor Development
Months 13—16

Your child's motor skills may develop so well that he is always in motion during months 13—16. Describe his progress in crawling, climbing and walking at start and end of this period.

At 13 months	At 16 months
Crawling:	Crawling:
Climbing:	Climbing:
Walking:	Walking:

A REMINDER: BABYPROOFING SHOULD CONTINUE. RE-READ THE CHART ON PAGE 60 AND UPDATE IT.

Check Your Progress
Months 13—16

At the end of month 16, read through what you've recorded in the learning charts. Think about the progress you and your child have made. How are things going? Is his development proceeding smoothly? Use the chart below to check your progress and plan how you can guide your child in the coming months.

Area of development	Progressing very well	Could be doing better	Use the spaces below to plan what you can do to assist your child's growth and development in the areas indicated.
	Check one		
Personality			
Use of mouth and eyes			
Use of fingers and hands			
Relationships with others			
Language			
Emotions			
Ability to move around			

Baby Talk

It feels good to know you well, Mom and Dad. Thanks for trying so hard to get to know me. I realize I've had you on the run. I couldn't do much for myself. I was too young to appreciate what you did for me. Now I'm old enough to feel your importance. I really count on you.

Since my first birthday I haven't been a very good companion. I've had temper tantrums. I've refused to do what you asked of me. I tested to see what I could get away with. Now I've learned there are limits and rules I must obey.

I'm going to improve during these coming months but I can't change overnight. I may be a little contrary for several more months. My improvement will be gradual. With your love and support I'll learn to behave in more acceptable ways.

During the next few months I'll improve in the following three areas: language, concentration and thinking.

I'll learn to talk. It takes time, but I'm trying. It's frustrating when I can't tell you in words what I want and need. I will be a good talker by the time I'm 2 years old. My grammar won't be much, but I'll know lots of words.

I'm learning to concentrate. I skip around from one activity to another now. Soon I'll spend long periods of time building with my blocks, looking at a book or putting puzzles together. I'm learning to focus my attention and be persistent. This will help my behavior, too.

My ability to think will improve. I'm learning to figure things out without having to experience them. Before, I needed to try something physically to understand it. But now I'll begin to understand things by thinking about them. When I'm about 2 years old, I'll

Learning to talk takes time. With your patience, your child will progress.

start calling on my memory. I'll use that knowledge to do my first real thinking.

Please don't expect too much too soon. I'll improve gradually.

Looking Ahead

What you've learned about your child during months 13—16 continues in this period. Your child's crisis between independence and dependence probably peaked at 16 months. While dependency is still a factor now, it will fade away gradually. *Independence will become dominant.*

During these eight months you may encounter refusals, tantrums and clinging behavior. But her development is increasing. You can look forward to better times.

Your child is maturing, but she still must have your consistent love and support.

GOOD TIMES AHEAD

You've devoted 16 months to your child. If you've worked hard, you can look for rewards during these months.

Don't give up when you find yourself tired. The future will be easier, especially if you concentrate on praising your child's successes. When she experiences fail-

Children need social activities with members of the family and with people outside the family. This toddler is learning to use a hammer as well as developing social skills. Exposure to older children is desirable, but you must protect your young child from fears and frustrations.

ure, divert her attention to another activity where she can succeed. Focusing on success and acceptable behavior is important. Your child needs to feel good about herself. Until her language improves, be patient and understanding with her speech.

SPECIAL NEEDS

Here are your child's special needs during this period:

Understanding Her Dependency Conflict—All your understanding and patience are required as your child's independence grows and she becomes less dependent on you. This conflict is a problem for her. Your awareness of it will make things easier for you both.

Language Development—Your child will need your help in learning to talk. She'll often learn new words at the rate of *one a day.* Don't expect grammar yet. This is a period of *labeling*, or relating objects to word meanings. Play lots of games for labeling. When you're dressing her, say, "This is a shirt." Let her repeat it. "This is an ear," and so on. She needs practice to increase her vocabulary. Sentences will come. *Now your child needs help with words as labels.*

Association with People—Your toddler needs to be around people and have experiences with them. You may have to arrange for this to happen. It's not too difficult if

you live in an urban or suburba environment. It may be hard you're isolated. Your child need experience with people *outside th family.*

Continue to protect your chil from fears and frustrations. Don let her bottle up emotion: Everyone has fears and everyon gets angry. The trick is to channe her emotions constructively. In struct your child to beat up pillow, not a brother or siste Teach her to hammer on a boarc not on you. Try to keep emotiona situations to a minimum.

Your child is an engaging littl creature. Enjoy these month when growth and development fi each day.

About Your Child

During months 17—24 your child should develop a good understanding of herself. Many words and statements are concerned with herself: "me," "mine," "me mean it" and "I do it myself." An 18-month-old child can be very forceful. This aggressive behavior is normal and gives you more opportunities to know your child.

Realize that your child is not *stable* in terms of her physical development and personality. Her personality is *changing,* sometimes expanding, sometimes contracting. This is closely related to the independency-dependency crisis. Every day is testing day. Your child tests her *capabilities* against all *possibilities* and *acceptabilities.* "Can I climb that ladder?" "Will Dad let me climb that ladder?"

MAKE YOUR REACTIONS CLEAR

A sign of progress will be apparent during these months. Your child will begin paying attention to your reactions. She may plan to grab a cookie, but first there is a swift glance at you. If you say "no," she may grab the cookie anyway. Her attention to you, slight as it may be, indicates she places importance on your reaction. This is a starting point. *Once you have your child's attention, be sure you make your approval or disapproval clear.* Your reactions are important to her and must be apparent without confusing her. She'll learn that when you approve, the results are more pleasant for her. Children are natural pleasure seekers.

You'll see other signs of progress. Your child will become interested in more complicated toys.

Your child does not have a stable personality. Personality changes and develops as your child grows. Every day is testing day: "Should I climb the ladder? Will they let me climb the ladder? Am I able to climb the ladder?"

Your youngster's activities with stuffed animals, toys, bedtime routines and other *regular* daily activities are part of her sense of *orderliness*. Rigid routines help satisfy her need for *security*. As a parent you can help by adhering to routines and encouraging orderliness.

Your toddler may not make the bed very well and may be in the way when you do household chores. But encourage and praise her attempts to help. It will boost her self-confidence.

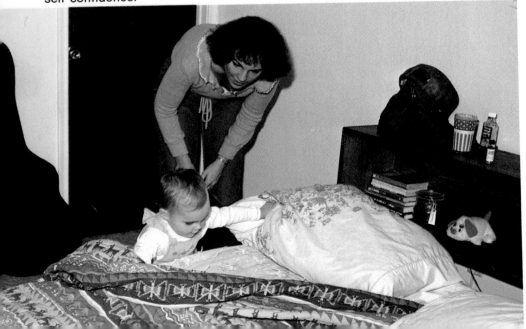

She'll devote more time to tasks. Watch her carefully to match tasks with her capabilities. *Don't exceed her pace, but challenge her.*

LET YOUR CHILD HELP YOU

If you don't have a copycat living with you, you soon will. Your child loves to imitate. Imitating you doing household tasks makes her feel grown up. Let her help you fold clothes, put away groceries and sweep walks. *Whatever the task, encourage her to become a helper.* Helpers feel good about themselves.

NEED FOR ORDERLINESS

There is a stage of *orderliness* that is important to most children. It has to do with daily routines and completion of tasks. "All done" is a common expression that indicates satisfaction. Your child will want to stick to her routines, often down to little details. Bedtime routines may be rigid. Every stuffed animal has its exact nighttime location. The book, truck and ball belong in a certain place. Then it's storytime or talktime. Next the bedcovers must be placed just so. The number of goodnight kisses and how they are given is predetermined. Omit one detail and you may be in for trouble.

Sense of Security—Why all this rigmarole? Routines and orderliness give your child a *sense of security.* As her world becomes more complicated, she requires security, depending on routines and exact places where things are kept. She deserves security in these months of rapid development. Follow routines. Encourage orderliness.

Changes are Confusing—Exploring the house goes along with the orderliness stage. Your toddler is struggling between independence and dependence. It helps to have something to count on. You

Brushing teeth is a habit your child should learn at this age. Encourage her and praise her. You may have to assist until she masters the skill.

home will be her security base. Keep things in place and stick to routines. She'll like helping you put clothes away. But if the underwear drawer suddenly contains sweaters, you may get a protest. *Change confuses and threatens her security.* Try to resist rearranging furniture for a few months. If changes are necessary, such as a family move, explain it to your child. Show her what changes have been made.

TEACH GOOD HABITS

The orderliness stage will not last forever. Teach her to pick up toys at this time. The habit will be more difficult for her to learn at a later date. A toy chest or shelf labeled with her name helps. At first you'll probably have to help her pick up. As you praise her for being a good helper, she'll gradually take over and do it alone. Emphasize how good you feel when she helps. Your helper will feel good, too.

Mouth and Eyes

Your child will have difficulty handling a cup. If she tilts it too much and too quickly, you can expect spills. Give her cups that are only half full. She'll still be messy, but she needs practice. Vary the kind of drink to encourage her to keep trying.

Using a spoon is tricky. Food always seems to drop off the spoon between plate and mouth. With practice your toddler will probably be an expert with cup and spoon by the end of her second year.

She may go through periods when she'll eat anything. At other times she'll be picky and selective. Mealtime will continue to be messy. As long as she hasn't developed eating problems, you can relax and follow her pace.

DEVELOPING CAUTION

In a few months she'll become more cautious. Situations, objects and people will be examined carefully before she takes action. She may just sit quietly and *watch*. She'll begin to understand spatial dimensions: up, down, over there, behind and ahead.

TIME FOR DENTIST

When your child has all 20 baby teeth, it's time to see a dentist. Even before this time, she'll want to use a toothbrush. She sees you or brothers and sisters brushing their teeth. It's a grown-up action and worthy of imitation. Watch her so you'll know when to buy her first toothbrush. Encourage her brushing to support her feelings of independence and self-confidence. You'll have to help her for several months. A 17-month-old child isn't very adept with a toothbrush.

117

Brushing and combing hair is a skill that comes slowly, sometimes comically. Your child's attempts indicate an interest in grooming. Encourage her.

Furniture, appliances and familiar sights in your home mean a lot to your child. Sense of security is closely tied to things known and seen regularly. When visiting another house, your child may be confused at the absence of familiar objects.

HAIRBRUSHING

Hairbrushing is another skill your child will want to learn. It can be comical, especially when she's looking in a mirror. A mirror image reverses right and left. That will confuse her. First attempts may cause more messing up than smoothing down. Encourage her attempts, but don't expect much. The skill will come gradually.

FAMILIAR SIGHTS

Your child will love to explore every article in the house many times. When visiting a strange house, she'll explore unless she's too shy. To her, house means a sofa, table, television set, bed, stove and so forth.

In a strange house, the absence of any of those items can be confusing. As she tries to think about what a house means, the lack of any item familiar to her can make a strange house bewildering. She'll need many experiences before she realizes houses are different. Her own home where everything is familiar will provide security.

Manipulation

The small muscles in your child's hands will become more developed during these eight months. Usually a child builds towers of three blocks at 17 months. By 24 months the child builds towers consisting of six or more blocks. Her ability to string large wooden beads will improve. She'll become more adept at pounding with a hammer and sorting shapes. Near the end of the year, she'll probably work with beads that snap together. She'll play with other complicated put-together toys. Small muscles will develop and greater finger dexterity will be possible.

THROWING IMPROVES

Progress will be made in throwing balls when her ability to release has improved. Your child will soon throw a ball and hit a target. It's important to her to make the ball do what she wants it to do.

FLEXIBLE WRISTS

Toddlers have wrists that are inflexible. Near the end of the second year the wrists loosen up. Finger dexterity increases. New activities can be learned that involve use of the hands. Watch your child turn the pages of a book. She'll turn several at a time. By 2 years of age, she'll probably be able to turn them one at a time. It's so much fun that she'll do this for long periods of time. She will pretend to read the book.

If you haven't done so, now is the time to give your child her very own books. *Cloth books or heavy cardboard books are best. She must learn that pages are not to be torn or removed.* This lesson is easier to teach if you have a stack of magazines that she is allowed to tear. Explain the difference to her.

Screwing lids on jars and turning doorknobs will become possible during these months. The wrist muscles must have time to develop. A helpful toy is a safe, well-made board with a number of latches, hooks, twist tops, knobs and switches. Another board can provide practice with zippers, buttons, hooks and eyes, snaps and shoelaces. If you're handy with tools, you can construct these boards at home.

DON'T CHANGE
HAND PREFERENCE!

You're probably still watching to see if your child is right-handed or left-handed. You'll notice preferences during these months. *By the second birthday* your child's choice of dominant hand will probably be obvious. *Don't change your child's hand preference. You risk confusing and possibly hampering later development.*

Choice of dominant hand may be uncertain until your child's second birthday.

Give your child books to look at, read or play with. This is helpful in the development of hand, wrist and finger skills.

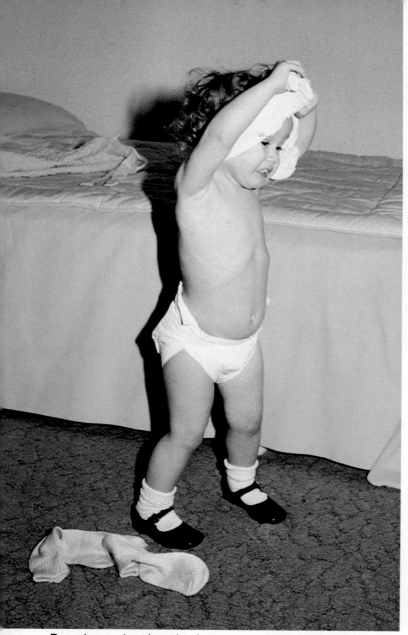

Dressing and undressing become easier as your child's muscles grow and dexterity improves. Your help may still be required until around 24 months.

DRESSING BECOMES EASIER

Dressing and undressing require small muscle control. Your child will become an expert at undressing during this period. Earlier, she resisted being dressed. *The resistance decreases at this stage and she actually cooperates.* She'll put out her legs for pants and drop her arms into armholes. Toward the second birthday, she may be able to put on her own pants. The right and left side and top and bottom of shirts will be a puzzle. Most children can use zippers well.

SCRIBBLING IMPROVES

The random scribbles of previous months will begin to take shape. Your child will first learn to draw vertical and horizontal strokes on paper with crayons. Then she'll draw a crude circular shape or even make a primitive V shape. This early art work is important. She's *creating* something. Your child will feel good about herself as she creates.

Display the Art Work—She may enjoy it when you display her art work. Refrigerator door, walls or table surfaces are good places to show her work. Your youngster will be delighted to get such attention and acclaim. Her self-confidence will increase. Frequent rewards give your child good feelings about herself.

Social Development

Your child's struggle between dependence and independence is important in her social development. Encourage her independence. But realize that the transition is not smooth. She knows that dependence on you is important. You'll see subtle and not-so-subtle demands for your attention. Your child still wants to be the center of attention. Once you understand her problem, it will be easier for you to be patient and supportive.

Things will improve by the end of this period. Your child probably will tolerate sharing your attention. Jealousy of a new baby in the family can be reduced. Allow your 2-year-old to help you with the baby. This is especially true if the toddler is made to feel *important* by helping.

SOCIAL ACCEPTANCE

Growth will occur in your child's social development. She has the ability to imitate and the desire to do grown-up tasks. She will now become aware of how you and others react to her.

Indicate approval when your child imitates you by waving and saying "good-bye." Praise her when she helps with the housework. But show your *disapproval* when your child says "no" to a reasonable request. She is sensitive to your reaction. You'll have to judge how to communicate disapproval without upsetting her. It may be as simple as saying, "I love you, but I did not like what you just did." She really wants to be socially acceptable. Your understanding and patience will help.

UNDERSTANDING POSSESSIONS

Your child is not old enough yet to share things that are hers. One reason is lack of experience. Before your toddler can truly share, she must understand the *concept of possessions.*

At this age your youngster's drive toward independence is becoming more obvious. It's not an easy change from depending on you. She still needs your attention and help.

Sharing toys is something your child won't be ready for at this age. The concept of **possessions must be understood first. That takes time and experience. Don't be concerned over your toddler's apparent selfishness. Playing will still lack direct involvement with other children. Keep an eye on these playtimes. Make sure they are pleasant experiences.**

At first she'll *hoard.* She'll grab everything in sight. This happens not because she really wants objects but because it feels good to have a lot. With your help she'll gradually learn that certain things belong to *her.* Then she'll learn what belongs to *you* and other members of the family. *Not until the idea of possessions is understood can your child move on to sharing.* Help her with the idea of possessions. Don't force sharing.

It becomes a struggle between two small children to see who will keep a prized toy. You can keep a *visitor's box* handy that contains toys for a visiting child. This way, your child doesn't have to share when she doesn't understand how or why.

PLAYING WITH FRIENDS

Playing with other toddlers will still be *parallel play* during months 17—24. Children seem unaware of each other much of the time, but they *are* aware. Each keeps track of what the other is doing. *They are not ready to interact directly.* One attempt at playing together may be grabbing a toy. The return reaction may be grabbing back or hitting. You should intervene if the interchange becomes too aggressive. You want these early playtimes to be as pleasant as possible.

Three's a Crowd—It's a good idea during these months to have your child play with only one friend at a time. Getting more than two young, inexperienced friends together is risky. It's too confusing for the children. *You must supervise* to ensure happy playtimes with a friend.

SHYNESS

At the end of the second year your child may go through another period of shyness. She feels secure with her family and friends. But strangers may make her uneasy. Don't push your child into social contacts. Divert attention away from her for the time being. Advances should come from your child. They will if you are patient and understanding.

SOCIAL NICETIES

More words will be learned. It will be time to teach "please," "hello," "good-bye," "how are you," "I had a nice time" and "thank you." At home you can teach the skills of being host and guest. Act out how to answer the door and how to answer the phone. Act out a visit ahead of time. Correct your child in a considerate way, but not in public. You want her to learn social skills, not feel ashamed or guilty. When she performs well, praise her. Progress comes gradually. Now your child is becoming the social creature you have wanted.

Language

Your child will begin paying closer attention when you talk. This is your cue to be a good model for her to imitate. Speak slowly and distinctly and *don't use baby talk.* Your child is also learning to appreciate the importance of language. *She's learning to get what she wants more efficiently by using words.* Her language development will be slower if you wait on her constantly. If you encourage the use of words, your toddler will try. Be patient. She may be frustrated and upset by her poor communication.

Getting what she wants by using words is a learning experience. Don't automatically wait on your child. When she indicates by gesture that she wants something, encourage her to speak her desires. But be patient.

PREPOSITIONS AND PRONOUNS

Single words come first, then two-word sentences that may be hard to translate. You must translate "come me" into "come with me" or "come to me." She'll learn prepositions such as "to," "with" and "on" by the end of this period. She'll use pronouns such as "I," "mine," and "yours," but not always correctly.

A NAME OF MY OWN!

Your toddler will also begin to refer to herself by name. This is a source of great satisfaction. You can help her by addressing her by name: "Lynn, please wash your hands." "Come to the table, Mary." Your child is old enough to recognize herself in snapshots. Play pointing and naming games with her. She'll love to hear stories where the central character bears her name.

A NAME FOR EVERYTHING

Another great step forward is when your child realizes that *everything* has a name. You'll constantly hear "What's that?" She's trying to learn names for things.

Labeling games are fun. Do this by pointing to body parts, articles of clothing and pictures in books. Ask for a name. Children love to be read to at this age and love to pretend to read. This helps them with labeling and word meanings.

SINGING AND DANCING

During this period your toddler will start singing and dancing. She'll love rhymes and jingles. She'll begin to show an interest in children's TV programs and commercials. *Hearing sounds, feeling objects, seeing things and acting out words are a part of language development.*

Your toddler's speech will show the sense of orderliness mentioned earlier on page 116. Phrases like "all gone" and "bye-bye" are *completion* phrases. They denote *the end of something.* This is important. It will add to her security and self-confidence. She'll learn to accept the completion of events.

TIME AND SPACE WORDS

Time words like "before," "after," "when," "then" and "soon" will appear. Your child will start to recognize the past, present and future. She'll understand the sequence of events. She'll remember past events and connect them to the present. She will learn more words of direction such as "under" and "over."

Emotions

Your child may exhibit emotional extremes during this period. She is a lovely, sociable person. What can be nicer than affectionate hugs and kisses? But sometimes she may be negative, demanding, aggressive and stubborn. She's expressing that conflict between independence and dependence mentioned earlier. Seeing and experiencing more will add confusion to your toddler's emotions. No wonder she has emotional ups and downs. Watch your child and try to understand what's going on in her mind. Then you can help her.

Put away complicated toys and puzzles. Make your requests simple. Some children can handle two requests at a time, others only one.

TEMPORARY REJECTION

Your child may occasionally reject you. You may be told to leave the room during mealtime. But listen for her whimper for help as she becomes tired or frustrated. Respect her individuality. But be ready to help when frustrations become unbearable.

NEW FEARS

Your child will develop new fears as she gets older. These may include fear of thunder, the dark, being left alone or of large animals. Fears of monsters and other imaginary creatures develop as her imagination grows and she is exposed to TV. Try to understand what frightens your child. Give her comfort and reassurance. You'll make matters worse if you try to force her to be brave. *Remember, you are her model of stability and security.* Her fears will gradually

You are your child's model of stability and security. But there will be times when you'll need attention yourself. If you are hurt or feel sad, your child may come to you with tenderness and a pat or kiss. She's too young to feel *sympathy*, but this display is the start of showing concern for others.

subside. If she wakes up frightened, reassure by hugs and kisses or a warm drink. A night light may help.

LEARNING SYMPATHY

Your child will probably begin to show *sympathy* toward others. When you get hurt, she may rush to pat you, kiss you or hug you. But she's still too young to sympathize. She's actually associating your hurt with her own welfare and security. It's a beginning of concern for others and contributes to her social development.

Motor Development

The energy of toddlers is incredible. Your child will seem to be always on the go. She'll slow down a bit near the end of her second year. Exercise is important as her muscles develop for walking, running, pushing, pulling, climbing and squatting. Perfecting her ability to move about helps her feel good about herself.

RUNNING AND JUMPING

You can expect your child to walk *backwards* and *sideways* during this period. *Running* will become smoother. She will have better control over stops and starts. But don't expect turning while running. That will come later. By the end of these months your child will probably be able to *jump with both feet, but not hop on one foot.* She'll probably *pedal* a small tricycle by 2 years of age and *throw overhand.* At first she'll *walk into* a ball, then gradually learn to *kick* it.

STAIRS

Skills for going up and down stairs differ for every child. Many 17-month-old children can go up stairs holding on to an adult's

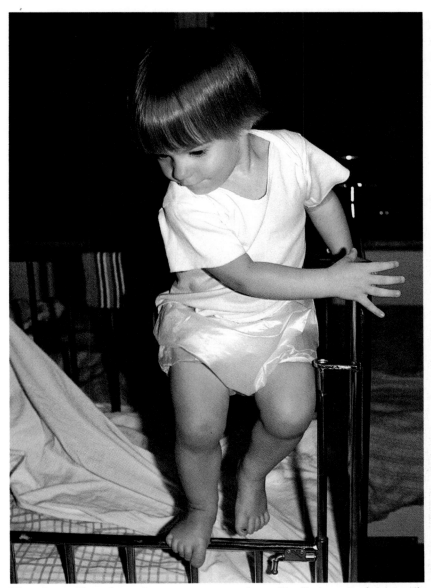

The day will arrive when your youngster will climb out of her crib unassisted, even when the rails are *up.* Then it's time to let her sleep in a bed. If your child is emotionally attached to her crib, be careful with this change. Don't rush. Proceed at her pace.

hand. Many will creep backwards to get down the stairs. Next, they learn to go up *and* down with adult help. Then the rail takes the place of the parent's hand. Finally, by 2 years of age, many children can be trusted to use the stairs on their own.

GRADUATING TO A BED

One day you'll discover that your child can climb out of her crib! That will be the time to think

about a bed. This can be an important growing experience.

Buy a regular bed. Junior beds are soon outgrown. You may want to get a detachable safety rail to make your child more secure.

Some children become emotionally attached to their cribs. It becomes their security location in the house. If this is the case, don't rush the move to a bed. Go at your child's own pace. Talk about how grown-up she'll be with her own full-sized bed.

Toilet Training

At first toilet training will be foreign to your child. She'll wet her diaper or have a bowel movement without control. It just happens and seems perfectly normal to her.

Your child will have no control until the last half of the second year. Even then the control won't be very good. Control depends on the development of certain muscles. This is a process that can't be hurried. You just have to wait.

Your child will have little interest in using the toilet before training begins. When you put her in the highchair, the reward is food for a hungry child. When you put her to bed, the reward is sleep for a tired child. When you put her on the potty seat, there is *no* reward. No wonder she isn't interested! You've taken away some of her playtime.

Toilet training begins when your child takes charge of her own bathroom behavior. She must be in control. Don't *impose* toilet training on her. You risk a battle. Let her take the lead in the whole matter. Consider what she must learn in order to control herself.

URINATION AND BOWEL MOVEMENT

As your baby grows, she'll discover that different parts of her body are parts of herself. She'll discover that urine and bowel movements come fro her body.

She might say "Wet!" as s points to a puddle on the flo She may be bare-bottomed the time and see the stream urine coming from her bo She'll begin to make the co nection between the pudd and herself.

THE POTTY CHAIR

Your child will learn th urine and fecal matter co out of her body. She must ne learn where to put them. Th is a difficult step for a sm child.

As far as she is concerne the only reason to use a pot chair is to please you. Toddl who want to show indepe

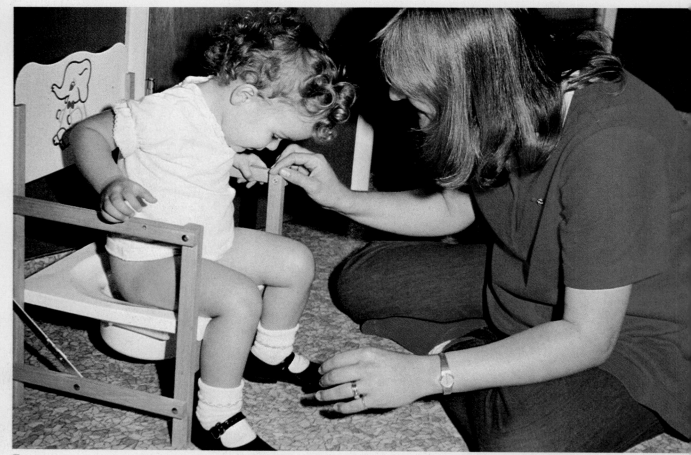

Encourage your youngster to use the potty chair. Encouragement should be gentle, without insistence. Your child m feel in control of the task.

dence may say "no" to any suggestion to sit in the potty chair. Keep it handy so your child will get used to it. *Don't force her to sit there.* Let her set her own pace. One day she'll gesture to you that she wants to sit in her potty chair.

YOUR CHILD WANTS TO PLEASE

At 24 to 30 months of age, children *do* want to please their parents. This is the best time for toilet training. Mother and father can demonstrate by their bathroom routines what they expect of the child. She'll gradually get the idea.

When she has her first bowel movement in the potty, congratulate her. But don't overwhelm her with praise. She may feel miserable later when she has accidents away from the potty.

EXPECT ACCIDENTS

You must *expect* accidents. Take them nonchalantly or you may make your child feel guilty. It will take many months before she is truly in control.

Control of the bowels usually comes first. Your child feels the physical warning signals several minutes before the event. The urge to urinate is followed almost immediately by urination. Your child can't get to the bathroom in time. Control of urination develops later.

BED WETTING

Staying dry at night is difficult for children. Use diapers at night until your child is ready and wants to sleep without them. *Don't expect this request until well beyond her third birthday.*

Try to understand how your child feels about toilet training. Let her train herself so she'll feel in charge. Your task is to give help where needed.

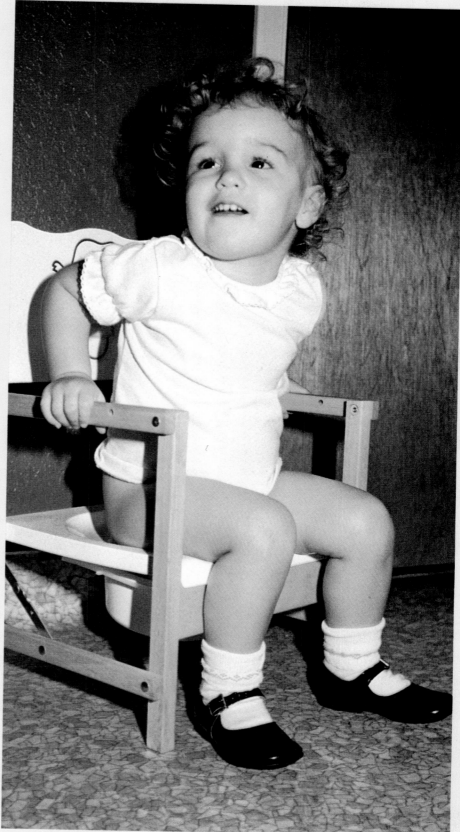

Your child will feel successful about toilet training if it is accomplished at her own pace.

127

Diary
Months 17—24

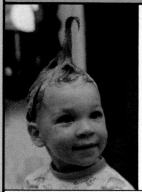

Use these diary pages to record significant events and developments in your baby's growth or behavior. These records can be useful in understanding your baby as she matures. They'll also be fun to re-read months or even years later. Get to know your baby!

Months 17—20:

Diary

Months 21—24:

About Your Child
Months 17—24

Your child will begin to understand what's expected of her during these months. Evidence of this will show up in her behavior. Describe your child's personality in the following areas.

What activities does she try only after first glancing at you for approval or disapproval?

List tasks or activities that your child frequently imitates:

What routines of orderliness does your child prefer at this age? See page 116?

Mouth and Eyes

Mealtimes will continue to be messy during this period. Your toddler may become skilled with cup and spoon by 24 months. At the end of this period, record her abilities below.

Holding and drinking from cup (Check one)	Messy, ☐ not adept	Does ☐ fair job	Neat, ☐ proficient
	Comments:		

Holding and eating with spoon (Check one)	Messy, ☐ not adept	Does ☐ fair job	Neat, ☐ proficient
	Comments:		

You may notice a real comedy when your child tries to brush or comb her hair in front of a mirror. This develops eye-hand coordination and good habits. Describe your child's hairbrushing:

Manipulation
Months 17—24

Your child may surprise you with hand and finger skills during this period. Describe how she handles the following tasks.

At 17 Months

Task	Performance
Building block towers	
Throwing ball	
Turning pages of book	
Twisting doorknobs, lids	
Undressing and dressing	
Art work	
Stringing or snapping beads	
Pounding with hammer	
Zippers and buttons	
Other	

Describe the same skill performance at 24 months of age and compare with above.

At 24 Months

Building block towers	
Throwing ball	
Turning pages of book	
Twisting doorknobs, lids	
Undressing and dressing	
Art work	
Stringing or snapping beads	
Pounding with hammer	
Zippers and buttons	
Other	

HAS YOUR CHILD SHOWN A HAND PREFERENCE? Right-handed ☐   Left-handed ☐   Don't know yet ☐

131

Social Development
Months 17-24

Months 17—24 may be the period when your child learns to speak and understand words of social grace. Record the dates your child learns social words. Describe how she understands and performs.

Word or task	Date learned	Level of understanding
"Please"		
"Thank you"		
"You're welcome"		
"Hello"		
"Good-bye"		
"How are you?"		
Answer the door politely		
Answer the phone politely		

Language

When you speak, your child will listen more carefully during this period. It's an important time to work on teaching new words and correct usage. *Remember: Don't use baby talk.* Keep a record below of some of your child's language skills.

Language	Date learned
Knows and uses her own name	
Knows and uses family members' names	
Sings and dances (concept of words put to music)	
Uses time words ("before," "after")	
Uses space words ("under," "over")	
Uses two-word sentences, or longer	
Uses prepositions ("to," "with," "on")	
Uses pronouns ("I," "you," "me")	

List objects that your child can call by name:

Emotions
Months 17—24

This will probably be a period of frequent emotional extremes for your child. She may be happy and affectionate one moment, then demanding and aggressive the next. Describe her emotional behavior below.

Do you occasionally find your child rejecting you for short periods? Describe, then answer question below:

How did you respond to your child when she temporarily rejected you?

Has your toddler learned sympathetic behavior? How does she act when she knows you've hurt yourself or when you're sad or upset? Answer here, then respond at right:

When your child showed concern or sympathy for you, how did you react to her?

Has your child developed new fears, such as fear of thunder, the dark, being alone? Describe, then answer at right:

How did you console your child when she showed fear?

Motor Development

Your child's ability to move about and do things may astound you during these eight months. Keep a record of her progress.

Skill	Date learned or progress made
Takes steps backwards	
Takes steps sideways	
Runs with smooth starts and stops	
Jumps with both feet	
Pedals tricycle	
Throws objects overhand	
Kicks a ball	
Climbs stairs safely alone	
Climbs out of crib alone	

Check Your Progress

At the end of month 24, read through what you've recorded in the learning charts. Think about the progress you and your child have made. How are things going? Is her development proceeding smoothly? Use the chart below to check your progress and plan how you can guide your child in the coming months.

Area of development	Progressing very well	Could be doing better	Use the spaces below to plan what you can do to assist your child's growth and development in the areas indicated.
	Check one		
Personality			
Use of mouth and eyes			
Use of fingers and hands			
Relationships with others			
Language			
Emotions			
Ability to move around			

Baby Talk

A number of months ago I promised you I would improve my behavior. Well, I'm not perfect yet, but I've improved quite a bit. It's my way of saying "thank you" for what you've done for me in 24 months. I'll no longer have temper tantrums, but I may slip once in a while. I've learned to say "yes" instead of "no" when you ask me to do something. I help around the house so our family will be happy.

I'm learning to do things you want me to do, not just the things I want to do. I can play with more complicated toys and puzzles without your help. Remember when I used to pester you constantly? You see, I really have improved!

I look forward to the coming six months. I will improve my skills. Two things are important to me now: getting to know you even better and trying to please you. Let's enjoy these six months together.

More complicated toys and tasks are suitable now.

Looking Ahead

You and your child have made great progress in the past two years. That cuddly little baby has become an active bundle of energy. Now he's mature enough to truly become acquainted with you. That wasn't possible earlier because he was so self-centered. His self-centered behavior will gradually subside, but you'll see evidence of it for a long time. At least you have made a beginning. Your child pays attention to you and wants your approval!

Your child is entering an age when imagination and make-believe are important to his development.

He will practice and perfect all kinds of skills in months 25—30. Progress will continue through his preschool years. His outstanding accomplishments by 30 months will be *development of language, growth of imagination* and *bowel control.*

IMAGINATION AND MAKE-BELIEVE

Imagination depends on the ability to *symbolize.* Your child will learn that a block can symbolize a train or a stick can represent a magic wand.

You need to encourage his use of imagination. Some parents mistakenly discourage make-believe. They think of make-believe as unreal. Your child's world will be dull if he lives only with reality.

We are humans and we have imaginations. We can be *creative* and enrich our lives.

Don't deny your child the right to such riches. Join in the fun and play make-believe with him. Get out blankets, help arrange chairs and build a cave. Improvise costumes and play dress-up. Help your child make puppets, or make up stories and act them out together.

SPECIAL NEEDS

Your child's needs are the same ones you've worked hard to fulfill for two years. They are *understanding, protection, opportunities to practice skills, reinforcement of successes* and *consistent discipline.*

The most crucial need is your steady, continued love.

Children have a remarkable ability to use their imagination, play make-believe and symbolize. Encourage this to help improve your child's creativity. Help your toddler with make-believe. Allow time for pretending.

About Your Child

During these six months your child will learn to feel comfortable about himself. This is quite a change from the confusion he has felt since he became mobile. A continual problem was the battle between independence and dependence. Now you can look forward to a time when independence will win the battle. Continue praising successes, minimizing failures and providing many opportunities for practicing skills. Your child will have self-confidence and feel good about himself at 30 months.

INCREASING SELF-CONFIDENCE

Your child will learn who he is and what he can do. With all his independence, he'll also know when he needs help. He'll come to you for advice and guidance. Language is no longer a barrier. He can understand explanations and instructions. Keep them simple and in words that he knows.

Mother and father are the most important people in the world during these months. Your child's main motivation will be to please you. Treasure these months when your help is really appreciated.

Mouth and Eyes

Your child's table manners will improve. He will have mastered drinking from a cup by the time he is 30 months old. Spills will be infrequent. He may need some help with spoon and fork, especially when he's tired. For the most part he can take charge.

Keep the atmosphere relaxed. Don't force him to eat and don't worry about his eating enough. Appetites vary from day to day.

TABLE MANNERS

The best way to teach table manners is by example. You decide

Table manners are best taught by example. Your child imitates what you do.

what manners are required. Your child will eventually imitate you. He wants to please you. Your own manners will set the standard for your child's behavior at the table. "Please pass the bread" may come out as "Pees pass bed." But it's a good attempt and deserves your praise.

Be patient about table manners. They develop over many months. Keep mealtime relaxed and fun.

TEETH
Your child will probably have all 20 teeth by 30 months of age. The second molars will come through about the second birthday. Brushing teeth is very important now. If you have not taken your child to the dentist, take him at this time. It's wise to identify dental problems as early as possible.

SEEING IS BELIEVING
Children look and learn. Sometimes they look intensely at something like a truck or a sign. They forget all else and actually fall down. Your child must study every new sight so he can fit it into his experience. Each new sight is cataloged in his memory. A new sight, such as a merry-go-round, may be confusing. He'll stare and stare, trying to make sense of what he sees. When he has looked enough, let him ride one of the horses with you beside him. He'll probably remember that the sight means fun next time he sees a merry-go-round!

MEMORIES
Many memories are stored in your child's mind. You'll be surprised when he points out remembered landmarks when you go on a trip. He's looking at his world, thinking about what he sees and trying to make sense of it.

Manipulation
Your child will develop *preferences* when he reaches for objects. He'll reach for preferred objects rather than ones that are nonpreferred. He'll also develop the ability to reach *under, over* and *around* obstacles.

Reaching and grasping are clues to your child's physical and mental growth. He'll still have difficulty releasing objects. He'll grasp too hard and release too completely. The muscles in his hands and arms have not completely developed. Ball games and building towers with blocks will help.

Vision is one of your child's links to memory. What he sees is filed away in his memory to be recalled later. As his experience increases, he will begin to make sense of his world.

Your child's mobility and ability to manipulate things may improve at different rates. He may do one thing well, and another poorly. You can help by watching him and selecting activities that are best for his skills. Whether crawling after a tortoise, playing in a tree or climbing on playground equipment, your child will develop better if you challenge him. Don't overwhelm him with complicated tasks.

FITTING THINGS TOGETHER

Your child will love to fit things together and take them apart. He will be able to work with different size objects. He may especially like small ones. He may be interested in lining things up, such as putting spoons in order or placing stuffed animals in line. This activity is the orderliness that gives him security and a sense of completing what he's doing. See page 116.

Your toddler's wrist muscles have developed so knobs can be turned easily and jar lids unscrewed with arm rotation. This skill indicates progress.

MATCH TOYS TO SKILLS

Your child may progress more rapidly in some hand skills than others. He may be adept with his drinking cup but clumsy in throwing a ball. Watch his progress for clues in selecting appropriate toys.

If he has difficulty in throwing a ball, let him play with a large one. As he learns to release the large ball, introduce smaller ones. If a form board with geometric shapes is too complicated, give him a board with just circles or fewer shapes.

Gradually increase the complexity of toys as you observe your child's progress. You can become expert at choosing appropriate toys by observing his behavior.

Drawing and Painting—If your child shows an interest in drawing, hang a sheet of paper on the wall. Draw a circle and see if he will imitate. Don't expect perfection. Most children of this age can draw only crude circles, squares and rectangles. Try finger paints and poster paints. One color at a time is enough at the beginning.

HAND PREFERENCE

Hand preference will probably be well established by this period. *A reminder: Don't try to change hand preference.* If you insist that your child change hands, you might interfere with nerve impulse patterns. This can lead to confusion. Some experts believe that *stuttering* can be caused by trying to change hand preference. It's safer to let your child decide naturally which hand he'll use. For more on stuttering, see page 144.

Social Development

Differences in social development will be exhibited during months 25—30. Your toddler may be generally aggressive or he may be shy and timid. Or he may be aggressive one moment and shy the next. Get to know your child. Then you can predict what social behavior to expect.

NOT ALWAYS CONSISTENT

Don't expect your child to be *consistent.* Remember the conflict between independence and dependence is still affecting him. He may be aggressive at home but cling to you when away. He may play quietly and be indifferent to his toy train on a shelf. But let another child touch that train and your toddler may scream, grab or hit.

Your child will sometimes *contradict* himself. He will struggle to make a choice. Once it's made he may reverse it. Think about how he sees life. He has little experience. He's just learning to do things for himself. He knows something about what you expect of him, but not much. When he says "no," he sometimes gets his way. But he also realizes how important *you* are when he's tired or frustrated. He can't do without you. It's pretty confusing. This is why he has his ups and downs.

Hand preference may be obvious by this age. One hand may be used for holding, while the dominant hand is used for manipulating. It's best to let your child decide naturally which hand to use.

Personality and social habits may be inconsistent during months 25—30.

IMPORTANT ROUTINES

There are some exceptions to your child's inconsistency. These have to do with his routines. There may be a regular ritual for going to bed, taking a bath and putting toys away. If anyone interrupts one of his rituals or changes part of a routine, he may become frustrated. He needs routines for security.

WATCHING OTHER CHILDREN

Your child will *watch* other children when he plays. Children watch each other and learn what to expect. It's important for your child's social development to have other playmates to observe. Playing *beside* another child is an *extension of watching*. Very few children in this period play with other child-

ren in a cooperative sense. But they learn as they watch and occasionally grab a toy or hit and kick. Remember, they can't share yet. But they do learn what is "mine" and what is "yours."

Don't rush your child's social development. Let him set the pace.

Language

It may seem that your child learns several words every day now. This rapid increase in vocabulary is normal during these months. Your child will also begin to learn grammar.

HOW DO THEY LEARN?

There are many theories about how children learn language. One

is that they learn by *imitating*. They repeat what they hear others say. These imitations are an important part of learning language. That is why you should speak slowly, clearly and correctly to your child.

Your child may say, "I *growed* up." He is not imitating but has *figured out a grammatical rule*, even though incorrectly. The past tense of grow is grew, but he is learning the general rule of adding the sound of "—ed."

LOCATION WORDS

Words that describe location become more important as your child explores. "Here" and "there" will have meaning. "Where" will enter your child's questions. Words like "home" and "work" (your job) will be un-

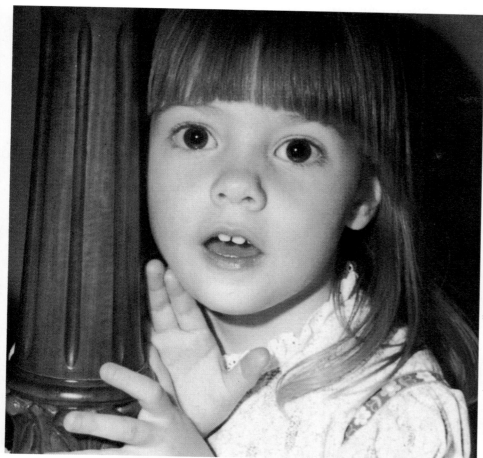

Language development may be rapid in this stage of life. Your child will build a vocabulary in many ways, such as playing with brothers and sisters or chattering over discoveries at the dinner table. Your child may advance from two-word sentences to longer sentences with some words missing. Help your child by communicating in simple but adult language.

derstood. Your child can learn about the meaning of space by hiding toys and then looking for them. Some children enjoy playing this game in the dark.

Your child will learn *up and down, back and forth, in and out, top and bottom* and *off and on.* Don't be surprised if he gets some of these reversed at first. You can set up situations to help him learn the meaning of these words. Tossing a ball up and down will help.

LONGER SENTENCES

Your child won't master language overnight. During this period you can expect two-word sentences to be replaced by longer sentences with some words omitted. "See truck, Mommy." Words will be used incorrectly.

A child needs to develop a sense of security, trust and self-confidence. These traits will come if you are dependable and loving in meeting your child's needs.

Frustrations may be the cause of *stuttering*, which is common at this age. There may be undue pressures on your child. Try to identify and reduce them. Jealousy of a new baby, a family move or a loved one departing are examples. *Don't be upset about stuttering. Don't try to correct your child.* A calm atmosphere is important during these months of rapid language development. Be considerate of him. You may have overstimulated him with too many word games, stories and too much talking. *Slow down. Stuttering will gradually subside.*

Emotions

Your child may be passive and unemotional. But it is more likely that you are living with a lively bundle of emotions all ready to explode. Children can do many things by themselves at this age. There will still be trouble with dressing and using a fork and spoon. But your child can move about freely and communicate in your language. He'll feel important. There will still be a strong sense of dependence along with his independence. Your child knows that getting along in this world would be impossible without you.

This need for a parent explains why some children panic when that parent leaves. Some children refuse to let the parent out of sight. This behavior is not likely to occur if you know your child. At age 2, children whose needs are met are secure enough to know that parents who leave will return. They'll understand that when you say "I will be back," you *will* be back.

AFFECTION

You can look forward to affection from your child during these six months. You've loved and supported your child for two years. He was too concerned with himself to take much notice of your reac-

"Me make bridge." Gradually "I" will replace the word "me."

DON'T LOSE PATIENCE

You may see your child struggling for the right way to start a sentence or express an idea. The desire to communicate is compelling. Unfortunately, some adults lose patience with a struggling child. They absent-mindedly respond with "uh-huh," with an interruption, or even worse, by walking away. This is upsetting to a child who wants to speak and is frustrated by words and grammar.

These six months can bring you a reward of affection from your child. Earlier, your child was probably too involved in personal needs to return much affection. Now your youngster may be very affectionate. A kiss for Mom or Dad goes a long way!

ions. Now you'll get your reward!

Your child is interested in your reactions. You're important in his eyes. One day he will see you tired and dejected, maybe even in tears. He'll come to you, hug you and give you a kiss. He can sense that something is wrong. He'll want to make things right. He's too young to understand your feelings. But his affectionate behavior is the beginning of sympathy.

FEAR OF BEING HURT

Another fear may be evident during these months. It has to do with your child's *physical well-being.* Now that he knows he is different from other people, bodily hurts are more threatening. He may worry about bleeding, being sick and getting hurt. He may even refuse a broken cookie or fear a handicapped person. He may associate them with what could happen to him. This is a subtle kind of fear. You may miss it unless you are aware that it can occur. *It must be acknowledged and dealt with. Don't let your child bottle up fears.* Help him with fears by discussing them. With your reassurance and explanations, his fears will subside.

Motor Development

These months will be filled with running, climbing, pulling, pushing, squatting and stooping. Take a good look at your child in a standing position. You'll probably see knees and elbows that are slightly bent. Shoulders may be somewhat hunched. The waist is more flexible. *Bending from the waist is becoming possible. He is better at stooping than squatting.* Watch how your child gets to an upright position. He leans forward, then raises his buttocks. Then his head comes up.

Your child may want to run, climb and do every other imaginable exercise. He may not be too graceful. But after all, he's still developing. This is a time to channel his energy into useful tasks.

Climbing on things is still a favorite pastime. *Jumping and bouncing* will begin during these months. Your child probably can walk along a low wall or a raised board with your hand support. By the end of this period, he may balance on one foot for about five seconds.

HOUSEHOLD HELPER

Physical activity can be directed to your advantage. There are many household tasks your child can do. Those tasks won't be done to perfection. Give your child a purpose for physical activities. He'll learn to be helpful. Observe carefully what he is able to do, then provide opportunities.

TOILET TRAINING

Toilet training will probably proceed in a relaxed manner during this period. See pages 126 and 127. Control of bowels is attained by most children during these months. But bladder control is usually more difficult. Many children stay dry at night only when they are about 3 years old.

When your child reaches the end of this period, you have another significant date to look forward to: *the third birthday.* Most 3-year-olds are a delight.

Your Child's Positive Self-Image

Children and adults who feel good about themselves are healthy, happy people.

You have to feel good about your life and about the people you work and associate with to maintain a positive self-image. That sounds complicated, and it is.

Your youngster's self-image depends on you. You have to help him build it. The ingredients for a young child are the same as they are for you. *Your child must learn to feel good about himself and his environment. He must feel good about the adults and other children around him.*

Your task will not be easy. You'll be called on to give a great deal. You must love and understand. When your child is 30 months old you'll receive affection in return. But you'll receive little understanding of your feelings.

You may *never* receive understanding from your child unless you help him develop his own positive self-image.

Get to know your child. Understand what he's trying to tell you. If his needs are met and he is treated as an individual, he'll develop a positive self-image. If his needs are not met, he may develop a neutral or even bad image of himself.

Helping your child develop a positive self-image will pay off in the long run for him as well as you.

Hard work, love, patience and understanding will pay off as your child grows older and develops a good self-image.

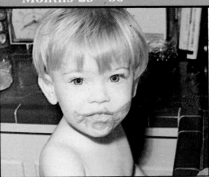

Use these diary pages to record significant events and developments in your child's growth or behavior. These records can be useful in understanding your child as he matures. They'll also be fun to re-read months or even years later. Get to know your child!

Months 25—27:

Diary

Months 28—30:

About Your Child

During these six months your child will develop greater self-confidence and independence. Describe activities that show he can do things for himself:

Mouth and Eyes

By this age your child has learned that certain behavior is expected at the dinner table. Describe his progress in table manners:

Your child's ability to see and remember things will develop rapidly. List places, such as stores, houses or landmarks, that your child knows by sight:

Manipulation
Months 25—30

Reaching and grasping are clues to your child's physical and mental growth. Describe his progress in holding, carrying, manipulating and releasing objects:

Fitting things together and taking them apart, such as working simple puzzles, are part of your toddler's *orderliness* training. What activities indicate your child's orderliness?

You are probably good at matching toys to your child's abilities. As you give him new toys, watch his behavior and rate the toys for suitability.

List of new toys	Too complicated	Just right	Too simple

Social Development

How has your child developed in his attitude toward others? Does he get along well with adults outside his immediate family? With other children? Describe:

Social Success Chart

What are the social situations in which your child enjoys himself most and gets along best with other people?

Some social situations may be unsuccessful for your child. What are they?

Language
Months 25—30

Now is a time of rapid vocabulary development for your child. Chart his word progress below.

New Word List					
Month 25	Month 26	Month 27	Month 28	Month 29	Month 30

Emotions

Your child may begin showing increased affection for you and others during this period. His self-centered behavior may decrease. How does he show affection?

Your child may fear getting hurt. Describe any fears about well-being that he shows. What did you do or say to help him cope with it?

Motor Development
Months 25—30

Describe your toddler's progress in motor skills.

Running:

Climbing:

Pushing and pulling:

Squatting:

Bending or stooping:

Other:

Household Tasks

What are tasks your child enjoys and willingly helps you with?	What are other tasks that you and your child can do together in the future as he develops his skills?

Check Your Progress

At the end of month 30, read through what you've recorded in the learning charts. Think about the progress you and your child have made. How are things going? Is his development proceeding smoothly? Use the chart below to check your progress and plan how you can guide your child in the coming months.

Area of development	Progressing very well	Could be doing better	Use the spaces below to plan what you can do to assist your child's growth and development in the areas indicated.
	Check one		
Personality			
Use of mouth and eyes			
Use of fingers and hands			
Relationships with others			
Language			
Emotions			
Ability to move around			

A cheery disposition and love for living things will result from your understanding and praise.

The Future

If you have come to know your child and if you communicate with each other, then you are prepared for the future. You can reach several goals when your child is 3 years old. With continued understanding and patience you can expect:

1. Completed toilet training.
2. Mastered self-help skills such as table manners and dressing and undressing.
3. Advanced mobility and hand skills.
4. Cooperative play with others, such as sharing and taking turns.
5. Helping around the home.
6. Persistence and concentration.

You and your child both deserve a pat on the back. You have laid the groundwork for your child's future. Now your youngster can take some of the initiative in learning and growing.

7. Plenty of imagination.

8. Requests for your advice and explanations.

9. Cheerful disposition.

10. Love and enthusiasm for learning.

Your child will be a joy to live with. You both deserve credit. Development started at birth when you and your baby began communicating and getting to know each other.

For many months the initiative was yours. Now your child has begun to do things on his own. You have built a relationship that prepares you both for the future.

Sources of Information

The following list of books will give you more to read about child development. The books offer information about working mothers, the father's role, childhood self-esteem, games, storytelling and learning to love.

These books are short, easy-to-read paperbacks written for parents:

Barber, Lucie W. *Celebrating the Second Year of Life: A Parent's Guide to a Happy Child.* Birmingham, Alabama: Religious Education Press, 1979.

Barber, Lucie W. *When a Story Would Help: An Approach to Creative Parenting.* St. Meinrad, Indiana: Abbey Press, 1981.

Chess, Stella; Alexander Thomas and Herbert G. Birch. *Your Child is a Person: A Psychological Approach to Parenthood Without Guilt.* New York: Parallax Publishing Co., Inc., 1965.

Losoncy, Larry. *When Your Child Needs a Hug.* St. Meinrad, Indiana: Abbey Press, 1978.

Olds, Sally Wendkos. *The Mother Who Works Outside the Home.* Child Study Press. Child Study Association of America—Wel-Met, Inc., 1975.

Smith, Helen Wheeler. *Survival Handbook for Preschool Mothers.* Chicago: Follett Publishing Co., 1977.

Thompson, Andrew D. *When Your Child Learns to Choose.* St. Meinrad, Indiana: Abbey Press, 1978.

These paperbacks are more detailed and addressed to both parents and professionals:

Biller, Henry, and Dennis Meredith. *Father Power.* Garden City, New York: Doubleday, Anchor Press, 1975.

Braga, Joseph, and Laurie Braga. *Growing With Children.* Englewood Cliffs, New Jersey: Prentice-Hall, Inc., 1974.

Briggs, Dorothy C. *Your Child's Self Esteem.* Garden City, New York: Doubleday and Co., Inc., Dolphin Books, 1975.

Leach, Penelope. *Your Baby & Child: From Birth to Age Five.* New York: Alfred A. Knopf, 1978.

McDiarmid, Norma J.; Mari A. Peterson and James R. Sutherland. *Loving and Learning: Interacting With Your Child From Birth to Three.* New York: Harcourt, Brace, Jovanovich, 1975.

Spock, Benjamin. *Baby and Child Care.* New York: Pocket Books, 1977.

These are hardback editions for parents:

Arnstein, Helene S. *The Roots of Love: Helping Your Child Learn to Love in the First Three Years of Life.* Indianapolis/New York: The Bobbs-Merrill Co., 1975.

Brazelton, T. Berry. *Infants and Mothers: Differences in Development.* New York: Delacorte Press, 1969.

Brazelton, T. Berry. *Toddlers and Parents: A Declaration of Independence.* New York, Delacorte Press, 1974.

Bricklin, Barry, and Patricia Bricklin. *Strong Family, Strong Child: The Art of Working Together to Develop a Healthy Child.* New York: Delacorte Press, 1970.

Gardner, George E. *The Emerging Personality: Infancy Through Adolescence.* New York: Delacorte Press, 1970.

Gordon, Ira. *Baby Learning Through Baby Play.* New York: St. Martin's Press, 1970.

Gordon, Ira. *Child Learning Through Child Play.* New York: St. Martin's Press, 1972.

Salk, Lee. *What Every Child Would Like His Parents to Know.* New York: David McKay, 1972.

Spock, Benjamin. *Raising Children in a Difficult Time.* New York: Norton and Co., Inc., 1974.

These hardcover books are mainly for professionals but will be of interest to parents.

Gesell, Arnold, and Frances L. Ilg. *Child Development: An Introduction to the Study of Human Growth.* New York: Harper and Brothers, 1949.

Lynn, David B. *The Father: His Role in Child Development.* Monterey, California: Brooks/Cole, 1974.

Thomas, Alexander, and Stella Chess. *Temperament and Development.* New York: Brunner/Mazel, 1977.

Index

A

About Your Child, Months 1 & 2, *8*
About Your Child, Months 3 & 4, *27*
About Your Child, Months 5—7, *46*
About Your Child, Months 8—12, *67*
About Your Child, Months 13—16, *91*
About Your Child, Months 17—24, *115*
About Your Child, Months 25—30, *138*
Accidents, *90, 127*
Accomplishments, *101*
Adult taboos, *76*
Affection, *49, 72, 144*
Age of the mirror, *46*
Aiming, *93*
Ambidextrous, *70*
Anger, *74, 101, 114*
Appetite, *92*
Apposing thumb, *48*
Approval, *53, 115, 121*
Art work, *79, 94, 120, 140*
Association with people, *114*
Attachment, *30, 66, 72*
Average child, *5, 90*
Awake, *43*

B

Babbling, *11, 31, 51*
Baby battles, *96*
Baby sitter, *33, 64, 100, 101*
Baby talk, *99, 123*
Babyproofing your home, *45, 60, 65, 67, 90*
Balance, *75, 93*
Ball games, *94, 139*
Balloons, *78*
Bathroom behavior, *126*
Beads, *118*
Bed wetting, *127*
Beds, *125*
Behavior, *53, 91, 141*
Bending from the waist, *145*
Bladder control, *146*
Blocks, *70, 78, 94, 95, 118, 139*
Body contact, *11*
Body language, *99*
Bonding, *7, 9, 10, 49, 72*
Books, *51, 119*
Bottle, *9, 26, 28*
Bowel movement, *126*
Boxes, *101*
Breast-feeding, *9, 25*
Brushing hair, *118*
Brushing teeth, *117*
Buttons, *119*

C

Cardboard books, *51, 119*
Cause and effect, *26, 49*
Changes in routines, *116, 117*
Charts, how to use, *5*
Childproof latches, *45*
Circles, *94*
Climbing, *63, 75, 101, 125*
Cloth books, *51, 119*
Clothespins, *101*
Comfort, *8*
Common discipline situations, *103*
Communication, *8, 10, 12, 51, 73, 98, 99, 100, 123*
Comprehension before speech, *73*
Concept of possessions, *122*
Concern for others, *124*
Connecting sight and sound, *28, 29*
Conscious learning, *10*
Consonants, *31, 51*
Contact with people, *50, 96, 97*
Cooing, *31, 51*
Crawling, *12, 45, 52, 63, 101*
Creativity, *120, 137*
Creeping, *125*
Crib, *125*
Cruising, *75*
Crying, *7, 8, 10, 11, 12, 26, 72, 74*
Cupboards, *64*
Cups, *92, 93, 101, 117, 138*
Curiosity, *27, 43, 44, 46, 49, 52, 64, 92*

D

Dancing, *124*
Danger, *13, 45, 65, 75*
Day care, *33*
Delayed learning, *75*
Dentist, *117, 139*
Dependability, *26*
Dependence, *100, 113, 114, 121, 138, 141*
Depth perception, *29, 47*
Desired behavior, *91*
Developing caution, *117*
Dexterity, *120*
Differences in children, *67*
Disapproval, *53, 115, 121*
Discipline, *65, 91, 102, 103, 137*
Dominant hand, *119, 141*
Doorknobs, *119*
Drawing and painting, *79, 140*
Dreams, *74*
Dressing, *120*
Dropping, *47, 49, 71*

E

Eating, *8, 29, 64, 68, 117*
Emotional attachment, *7*
Emotions, Months 1 & 2, *12*
Emotions, Months 3 & 4, *31*
Emotions, Months 5—7, *52*
Emotions, Months 8—12, *74*
Emotions, Months 13—16, *100*
Emotions, Months 17—24, *124*
Emotions, Months 25—30, *144*
Energy, *43, 46, 90, 137*
Examining food, *68*
Exploring, *27, 28, 47, 49, 52, 63, 64, 66, 90, 118, 142*
Exploring hand, *70*
Eye-hand coordination, *30, 47*

F

Faces, *9, 10, 11, 25, 31, 46, 49, 69, 72*
Failure, *101, 113, 114*
Falls, *13, 45*
Fascination objects, *29*
Fascination with faces, *9*
Fascination with small objects, *47*
Father's role, *14*
Fear, *11, 12, 31, 64, 74, 91, 100, 114, 124, 145*
Fears learned from experience, *100*
Fears learned from other people, *100*
Feeding, *25, 26, 68, 92, 117*
Feeling, *66, 69*
Finger paints, *140*
Fingers, *30, 51*
First step, *75*
First teeth, *48*
First word, *73*
Fitting things together, *140*
Flexible wrists, *119*
Fondling, *76*
Food, *28, 44, 47*
Form board, *94, 101, 119, 140*
Frustration, *32, 71, 74, 78, 91, 101, 114, 123, 144*
Future, *156*

G

Games, *50, 66, 68, 93, 94, 97, 114*
Gates, *45, 63*
Gazing, *10*
Genitals, *76*
Geometric shapes, *101*
Gestures, *98, 99, 100, 123*
Goals, *49*
Grammar, *73, 114, 142*
Grasp reflex, *10, 48*
Grasping, *48, 49, 52, 69, 139*
Guilt, *77*
Gums, *48*
Gumming, *28*

H

Habits, *117*
Hairbrushing, *118*
Hand preference, *95, 119, 141*
Handling objects, *66*
Hands, *10, 30, 51, 70, 119*
Hoarding, *122*
Hooks and eyes, *119*
Household tasks, *146*
Hunger, *11, 26*

I

Imagination, *79, 137, 138*
Imitation, *28, 46, 52, 71, 73, 97, 99, 116, 117, 139, 142*
Inconsistent behavior, *141*
Independence, *66, 67, 92, 113, 115, 117, 121, 138, 141*
Individuality, *67*
Injury, *45*
Intentional looking, *93*

J

Jargoning, *73*
Jealousy, *101, 121, 144*
Joy, *52*
Jumping, *125*

K

Knobs, *119*

L

Labeling, *114, 123*
Lamps, *45*
Language, Months 1 & 2, *10*
Language, Months 3 & 4, *31*
Language, Months 5—7, *50*
Language, Months 8—12, *73*
Language, Months 13—16, *97*
Language, Months 17—24, *123*
Language, Months 25—30, *142*
Latches, *119*
Laughing, *97*
Learn from experience, *43*
Left-handed, *70*
Leg strength, *32*
Lifts and collapses, *52*
Limits, *67*
Listening, *100*
Locomotion, *52*
Looking Ahead, Months 1 & 2, *7*
Looking Ahead, Months 3 & 4, *25*
Looking Ahead, Months 5—7, *43*
Looking Ahead, Months 8—12, *63*
Looking Ahead, Months 13—16, *90*
Looking Ahead, Months 17—24, *113*
Looking Ahead, Months 25—30, *137*
Looking behind, *92*
Love, *74, 113, 137, 147*

M

Magazines, *119*
Make-believe, *79, 137, 138*
Making mistakes, *7*
Manipulation, Months 1 & 2, *10*
Manipulation, Months 3 & 4, *29*
Manipulation, Months 5—7, *48*
Manipulation, Months 8—12, *69*
Manipulation, Months 13—16, *93*
Manipulation, Months 17—24, *118*
Manipulation, Months 25—30, *139*
Manners, *139*
Masturbation, *76*
Mealtime, *30, 68, 117*
Memory, *43, 49, 139*
Midline position, *32*
Mirror, *46, 97, 118*
Mobiles, *9*
Mobility, *32, 45, 52, 63, 64, 140*
Months 1 & 2, *7*
Months 3 & 4, *25*
Months 5—7, *43*
Months 8—12, *63*
Months 13—16, *89*
Months 17—24, *113*
Months 25—30, *137*
Moods, *52*
Moro reflex, *12*
Motor Development, Months 1 & 2, *12*
Motor Development, Months 3 & 4, *32*
Motor Development, Months 5—7, *52*

Motor Development (cont.)

Motor Development, Months 8—12, *74*
Motor Development, Months 13—16, *101*
Motor Development, Months 17—24, *125*
Motor Development, Months 25—30, *145*
Mouth and Eyes, Months 1 & 2, *9*
Mouth and Eyes, Months 3 & 4, *28*
Mouth and Eyes, Months 5—7, *47*
Mouth and Eyes, Months 8—12, *68*
Mouth and Eyes, Months 13—16, *92*
Mouth and Eyes, Months 17—24, *117*
Mouth and Eyes, Months 25—30, *138*
Muscles, *12, 32, 52, 74, 75, 94, 118, 120, 125, 139*

N

Names, *73, 123*
Nearsighted vision, *9*
Needs, *8, 11, 26, 44, 65, 90, 114, 137*
Nested plastic bowls, *101*
Nightfright, *74*
"No," *65, 115, 121, 126*
Nonverbal communication, *51, 98, 99*
Nursing, *11, 28*

O

Object permanence, *68, 69*
Opportunities, *26, 137*
Orderliness, *116, 124, 140*

P

Pain, *11*
Parallel play, *96, 122*
Parenthood, *5, 14*
Patience, *144*
Perception, *90*
Personal relationships, *66*
Personality, *8, 9, 27, 115, 142*
Physical care, *7*
Pillows, *78*
Place-holding, *29*
Plastic laminated books, *51*
Play, *96, 122*
Playpen, *32, 52*
Pointing, *75*
Possessions, *121, 122*
Possessiveness, *67, 72*
Poster paints, *141*
Pots and pans, *78*
Potty chair, *126*
Praise, *53, 71, 78, 117*
Preferred hand, *70*
Prepositions, *123*
Pretending, *138*
Pronouns, *123*
Protection, *45, 90, 137*
Pulling, *125*
Punishment, *77, 102*
Pushing, *125*
Puzzles, *101*

Q

Quality time, *33*

R

Rage, *31*
Raised head, *32*
Reaching, *69, 139*
Reactions, *115*
Reading, *51*
Reasoning, *90*
Records, how to use, *5*
Reflexes, *10, 12, 13, 27, 28, 48*
Refusals, *113*
Rejection, *124*
Release, *48, 93, 119, 140*
Repetition, *51, 71*
Responses, *26*
Restraints, *67, 101*
Reward good behavior, *92*
Right and wrong, *53*
Right-handed, *70*
Ritual, *142*

Index

R cont.
Rocking, *11, 30*
Role models, *77, 124*
Routines, *116, 142*
Rules about discipline, *103*
Running, *125*

S
Safety, *13, 45, 60, 65, 67, 75, 78, 90, 125*
Scanning, *92*
Schedule, *8, 65, 72*
Scooting, *52, 63*
Screwing lids, *119*
Scribbling, *79, 94, 120*
Security, *30, 72, 116, 117, 118, 122, 124, 125, 140, 144*
See and learn games, *93*
Selecting toys, *78, 79*
Self-confidence, *117, 120, 138, 144*
Self-discipline, *102*
Self-feeding, *44*
Self-image, *147*
Selfishness, *122*
Sense of humor, *97*
Senses, *11*
Sensorimotor skills, *48*
Sensory learning, *92*
Sentences, *123*
Separation anxiety, *72*
Sex identity, *76, 77*
Shapes, *118*
Sharing, *122*
Shoelaces, *119*
Shyness, *50, 71, 72, 122, 141*

Sights, *9, 28, 29, 93, 118*
Singing, *124*
Single words, *123*
Sleep, *8, 10, 25, 43*
Smell, *101*
Smiles, *10, 25, 26, 30, 31, 50*
Snaps, *119*
Social Development, Months 1 & 2, *10*
Social Development, Months 3 & 4, *30*
Social Development, Months 5—7, *49*
Social Development, Months 8—12, *71*
Social Development, Months 13—16, *95*
Social Development, Months 17—24, *121*
Social Development, Months 25—30, *141*
Sounds, *31, 51, 73*
Sources of information, *158*
Space perception, *47*
Space words, *124*
Special Needs, Months 1 & 2, *8*
Special Needs, Months 3 & 4, *26*
Special Needs, Months 5—7, *44*
Special Needs, Months 8—12, *65*
Special Needs, Months 13—16, *90*
Special Needs, Months 17—24, *114*
Special Needs, Months 25—30, *137*
Special relationship, *25*
Speech patterns, *73*
Spoiling your child, *7, 8, 102*
Spoons, *68, 93, 101, 117, 138*
Squares, *94*
Squatting, *125*
Stability, *124*

Stacking, *70, 75, 78, 94, 95, 118*
Stairs, *125*
Standing, *101*
Staring, *9, 10, 139*
Startle reflex, *12, 13*
Stranger anxiety, *71, 72*
Strangers, *31, 95, 122*
Stuttering, *141, 144*
Success, *114*
Sucking, *9, 28*
Swallowing, *28*
Switches, *119*
Symbolizing, *137, 138*
Sympathy, *124, 125*

T
Table manners, *138, 139*
Talking, *73, 98*
Tantrums, *74, 113*
Tasting, *68, 92, 101*
Teeth, *48, 50, 68, 117, 139*
Temper, *102*
Testing, *15, 68, 115*
Throwing, *47, 49, 71, 75, 93, 94, 119, 140*
Time words, *124*
Toilet training, *65, 126, 127, 146*
Tonic neck reflex, *13, 30*
Toothbrush, *117*
Touch, *48, 49, 52, 66, 69*
Toys, *26, 48, 68, 78, 79, 101, 116, 118, 119, 122, 140*
Trusting, *7, 144*
Twist tops, *119*

U
Understanding, *90, 137, 147*
Undesired behavior, *91*
Undressing, *120*
Union College Character Research Project, *5*
Urination, *126, 127*

V
Vases, *45*
Vision, *9, 28, 29, 47, 48, 68, 91, 139*
Visually directed reaching, *47*
Vocabulary, *28, 90, 98, 143*
Voices, *10*
Vowels, *31, 51*

W
Walking, *12, 45, 52, 63, 65, 75, 98, 101, 125*
Warning signals, *127*
Watching other children, *142*
Wooden beads, *118*
Words, *73, 99, 123, 124, 142*
Working mother, *33*
Wrists, *119*

Z
Zippers, *119*
Zwieback bread, *48, 68*

Charts

How to use, *5*
Months 1 & 2
 About Your Child, *18*
 Check Your Progress, *23*
 Diary, *16, 17*
 Emotions, *21*
 Language, *21*
 Manipulation, *20*
 Motor Development, *22*
 Mouth and Eyes, *19*
 Social Development, *20*
Months 3 & 4
 About Your Child, *36*
 Check Your Progress, *41*
 Diary, *34, 35*
 Emotions, *40*
 Language, *39*
 Manipulation, *37*
 Motor Development, *40*
 Mouth and Eyes, *36*
 Social Development, *38*
Months 5—7
 About Your Child, *56*
 Check Your Progress, *61*
 Diary, *54, 55*
 Emotions, *59*
 Language, *58*
 Manipulation, *57*
 Motor Development, *60*
 Mouth and Eyes, *56*
 Social Development, *57*
Months 8—12
 About Your Child, *82*
 Check Your Progress, *87*
 Diary, *80, 81*
 Emotions, *86*
 Language, *85*
 Manipulation, *84*
 Motor Development, *86*
 Mouth and Eyes, *83*
 Social Development, *84*

Months 13—16
 About Your Child, *106*
 Check Your Progress, *111*
 Diary, *104, 105*
 Emotions, *109*
 Language, *108*
 Manipulation, *107*
 Motor Development, *110*
 Mouth and Eyes, *106*
 Social Development, *107*
Months 17—24
 About Your Child, *130*
 Check Your Progress, *135*
 Diary, *128, 129*
 Emotions, *133*
 Language, *132*
 Manipulation, *131*
 Motor Development, *134*
 Mouth and Eyes, *130*
 Social Development, *132*
Months 25—30
 About Your Child, *150*
 Check Your Progress, *155*
 Diary, *148, 149*
 Emotions, *153*
 Language, *153*
 Manipulation, *151*
 Motor Development, *154*
 Mouth and Eyes, *150*
 Social Development, *152*

Acknowledgments

We would like to thank the following children whose photographs appear in this book:

Jennifer Babcock, Angela Barbee, Brandy Barnett, Jennifer Barnett, Raymond Bernaz, India Blatt, Elson Blunt, Brian Bosart, Keith Brady, Laura Brown, Johnnisha Lashonda Burton, Stacy Caughey, John Collier, Jeffrey Crookes, Richard Davis, Dana Derickson, Matthew Doberman, Bobby Dragoo, William Durning, Tyg Eagle, Jennifer Ensign, Aarron Feinberg, Jennifer Feinberg, Joshua Feinberg, Amy Gendron, Robert Michael Gennett, David Greenwald, Andy Grey, Margie Hendricks, Beth Hogan, Gregory Holzhauer, Thomas Huisking, Aline Jatulis, Tommy Jatulis, Matt King, Tara King, Brooke Malia Klinger, Brenda Loomis, Michael Andrew Lowry, Deborah Martinez, Kelly Mather, Betsy Medak, Ryan Millard, Becky Minnick, Sharron Minnick, David Mount, Sarah Mount, Suzette Munoz, Matt Redder, Kevin Shea, Michael Shiffler, Tom Shiffler, Kelsy Sloyan, Sean Strait, Stefan Strait, Robert Strittmatter, Blake Summerlin, Leyton Summerlin, Samantha Summerlin, Rachel Szalay, Elena Townsend, Tara Warfield, Karen Weaver, Nancy Weaver, Andrew Weigel, Sean Wellman, Joni Wilson, Ryan Woon, Sara Worthington, Benji Wright, Bridget Zwack.

A-5.6435137755